# James Renforth of Gateshead

# James Renforth of Gateshead

## Champion Sculler of the World

Ian Whitehead

Tyne Bridge Publishing

Acknowledgments:

No work of this type can be completed without the assistance of all kinds of people and this book is no exception. I am most grateful to Dilys Harding and the staff of Newcastle City Libraries Local Studies, where I carried out most of my research. Thanks also are due to Tyne and Wear Archives, Tyne and Wear Museums, Eileen Carnaffin, Anthea Lang and the Local Studies team at Gateshead Libraries. John Gall of Beamish Museum has taken a friendly interest in the work, sending interesting snippets of information through at regular intervals. John Lambert, of Tynemouth Rowing Club kindly allowed me access to the club's accounts. Christopher Dodd, of the River and Rowing Museum at Henley, encouraged me in my work. David Clasper, a descendant of the celebrated Tyne oarsman, Harry Clasper, provided a number of images of professional rowing on the Tyne.

Thanks are also due to Bill Miller for Canadian photographs, Les Golding for his excellent photography, Charlotte Harris, Ron French and William Spencer for historical research, and Carolyne Darling for reading the manuscript. Roy Watson and Martyn Chape produced fine maps of the courses on the Tyne, at Lachine, and at St John.

Finally I wish to say a big thank you to my daughter, Vita, who good-humouredly watched as an idea turned into a time consuming writing project, but never complained. Her clear-sighted remark when I was at first unable to find a publisher, 'Well, that's three years wasted!' served to keep my feet firmly on the ground. Now that I have a publisher I hope she has changed her mind about those particular three years.

*Ian Whitehead, 2004*

©Ian Whitehead, 2004

Published by
City of Newcastle upon Tyne
Education & Libraries Directorate
Newcastle Libraries & Information Service
Tyne Bridge Publishing
2004
www.tynebridgepublishing.co.uk

ISBN 1-85795-107-7

Printed by Elanders Hindson, North Tyneside

# Contents

# Preface

The origins of this book go back to a conference on the ancient Athenian Trireme, held at the River and Rowing Museum, Henley, in 1998. When Dr John Hale, of the University of Louisville, Kentucky, displayed an image of a print he owned of James Renforth in his skiff on the Tyne, I was surprised that a picture of somebody, whom I regarded as very much a Tyneside local hero, should be valued thousands of miles away in the USA. John kindly gave me the slide to pass on to Tyne and Wear Museums and I thought I would show my gratitude by sending him some pertinent biographical details from Renforth's home town.

A visit to Gateshead Libraries revealed that, although information on Renforth had been systematically collected in local history files over many years, a comprehensive biography of the rowing hero had never been written. After some encouragement from the then Local Studies Librarian, Eileen Carnaffin, I decided to attempt to fill the gap.

To begin with I had envisaged that there would only be sufficient evidence to write a shortish pamphlet, making the most important and interesting events of James Renforth's life available to the general reader. However as work progressed I began to feel responsible for ensuring that full justice was done to my subject. James Renforth was a man who struggled to express himself even when speaking to his fellow Geordies and who was too poorly educated to be able to set his thoughts down on paper. It was up to me to remedy the situation as best I could.

It is a dramatic and tragic tale, but I am an historian by trade, and by inclination, so my first duty was to tease out all the strands of the story. I hope that, as well as following the ups and downs of James Renforth's life, anybody reading this book will gain a good idea of how professional rowing was conducted in the 19th century.

Renforth was known as 'Jim' by his family and friends, but used 'James' when it was to be written and when conducting formal business. As a convention, therefore, I have used 'James' except when Renforth is being spoken to, or about, by his friends or family.

*A detail from a portrait of James Renforth sculling on the Tyne. Newcastle and the High Level Bridge can be seen in the background.*

David Clasper

*Rowing boats lie at the edge of the Tyne at Pipewellgate, Gateshead, c.1879.*

# A stone's throw

If you go to Gateshead and station yourself on the south bank of the River Tyne, at Pipewellgate, between the High Level and Redheugh Bridges, close enough to the river to throw a stone into the water, you will be standing where James Renforth spent his childhood. He was one of the greatest oarsmen and scullers of all time but you will find no commemorative plaque, no museum of rowing or Renforth 'Experience'. He is largely forgotten by the natives of Tyneside, who might remember that Harry Clasper was a famous Tyne rower, and, if pushed, that they have seen a funny, overly dramatic monument outside the Shipley Art Gallery, Gateshead, but few can recall whom it commemorates. There is a street named after him in Dunston, close to where he trained, but in Dunston nobody knows why it is so called. In New Brunswick, Canada, where he died, there is a town which bears his name.

Let us return to the Gateshead bank of the River Tyne and look over the safety rail at the water as it ebbs and flows, swirling and eddying around the bridge piers with just an occasional piece of flotsam drifting with the tide. River traffic is rare and you can count yourself lucky if you sight a police launch or some other small craft making its way up or downstream. But it was not always like this. In 1850 the Tyne was a busy, watery highway, with goods of all kinds being transported both up and down river. But the dominant feature was the constant movement of loaded keels and wherries, working the tides to carry seawards the coal which drove the industrial revolution. It was this bustling and ever changing scene which met the gaze of the young James Renforth.

But it was not only industrial traffic which passed by the tenements and cottages of Pipewellgate. By the time Renforth was a boy, the Tyne had become an established centre for professional rowing. Tynesiders were proud of their rowing traditions and, even after Renforth had become champion and was known across the world, he liked to be on the water in a racing boat whenever the customs of the river required it. He would have heard tales of the great races of the past, but compared to the Thames the history of boat racing on the Tyne was a relatively short one. While the London river could boast of having staged its first regatta in 1775, it was not until 1821 that the first official boat races were organised on the Tyne.

In that year, to celebrate the coronation of George IV, Newcastle Corporation promoted a boat race and offered four cash prizes, with Trinity House adding a blue silk flag for the winner. Thirteen boats were entered but when Coronation day, 19th July 1821, came, there was no race. Twelve of the competitors refused to take part because the North Shields boat, the *Experiment*, had been built especially for the race. The Coronation Committee awarded the first prize to the *Experiment*, while Trinity House decided that the race was null, and fixed a new date, the anniversary of the Battle of the Nile, 1st August, for a contest among the boats that had been entered – with the exception of the *Experiment*.

Six boats started on that day, with the Stella boat, the *Laurel Leaf*, winning the blue flag and the first three boats home picking up the three cash prizes which had not been awarded on Coronation Day. In 1830, a year after the first of the University boat-races on the Thames, the first races associated with the Ascension Day ceremonies on the Tyne took place. Annually, on Ascension Day, or 'Barge Day' as it was known, the corporate body of Newcastle, together with the Brethren of the Trinity House and guests and friends, used to 'beat the boundaries' of their jurisdiction on the river in a convoy of state barges, gaily decorated pleasure boats and bunting covered steamers. However, added to the ceremony in 1830 were horse races on the King's Meadows island and a regatta on the river, on Ascension Day, and on the day before and on the day after. Professional rowing on the river Tyne stemmed from this first Ascension Day regatta.

Having set the scene for the development of professional rowing on the Tyne, it would take a book in itself to do justice to the struggles for supremacy between the Claspers, the Taylors and the Elswick crews in the four oars, and the wonderful sculling careers of Harry Clasper and his protégé Bob Chambers, not forgetting Bob Cooper. And that would be without telling the story of Harry Clasper's development of the outrigger to make it a practical, working device or chronicling his boatbuilding advances which led to the production of the first proper racing shells.

Suffice it to say that the young Renforth would have seen for himself, and heard tales of, many famous races as he grew up on the south bank of the Tyne. However he was not a Clasper or a Taylor: he was not born into a rowing family. The work his father, and he himself did, did not naturally lend itself to a career in professional rowing.

Renforth was born on 7th April 1842 in a house in New Pandon Street, in the Manors district of Newcastle upon Tyne. The family connections were really with Gateshead and every contemporary biographical sketch says that he was born at Rabbit Banks, Gateshead, which is just a bit higher up the river bank than Pipewellgate. A later account of the Renforths' movements given by a younger brother, John, says that the family moved to Rabbit Banks when James was just one year old,

*An early painting of Harry Clasper sculling on the River Tyne. The Tyne Bridge of 1781, the demolition of which set Renforth on his way as an oarsman, is visible in the background. The High Level Bridge, which was opened in 1849, has yet to be built.*

which is probably what gave rise to the conflicting accounts of his place of birth. The official birth register and the entry in the 1851 Census record have him down as having been born north of the river, in Newcastle, and, with his brother John supporting this version of events, the evidence for a Newcastle birthplace is overwhelming. James's brothers and sisters were all born south of the river, and the 1851 Census records that the then eight year old James shared a cottage on Pipewellgate, Gateshead, with his father James, an anchorsmith, mother Jane, brothers Thomas, eleven, Stephen, four, and sister Mary Ann, three months.

His family was poor and in his youth he found work as a smith's striker at the North Eastern Railway Company's Engineering shops at Gateshead's Greenesfield works, at The River Tyne Commissioners Yard, Howdon, and at other engineering works on both the north and south banks of the Tyne. Similar concerns operated on both banks of the Tyne to supply the needs of the railways, mines and shipyards, and Renforth worked at a number of them. Manual workers were forced to move around by the operation of the 'market' system of hiring labour. Men seeking work waited outside the gates and were hired and laid off as dictated by the state of a company's order book. His father, also James, was an anchor smith and other members of the extended Renforth family were similarly engaged in smithing work.

Iron and engineering works came under scrutiny in 1842 when the Children's Employment Commission was investigating the effect of work on the lives of children. Evidence was taken from owners, overseers and children as to what life was like for the child workers of heavy industry. This provides us with a clear picture of the sort of conditions Renforth was to experience when he began work at what seems likely to have been perhaps age 11. We know from the Census of 1851 that his older brother Thomas was working as a labourer at age 11 but that James had not yet begun work at age eight.

A general description of the working lives of the children employed in an iron works drawn directly from the Commission Report shows what life would have been like for the young James Renforth.

### Children's Employment Commission 1842 (page 687)

**No 528 – At Messrs Crowley and Cos. Works at Swallwell, no evidence of a decided character relative to the effects of the labour upon the physical condition of the boys could be determined. It would seem however, in conjunction with much of the service of iron works in general, to be, if exercised within certain limits, conducive to muscular development, and the preservation of health. The business is carried on, as usual, daily for 12 hours, inclusive of one hour and a-half for meals; and at the rolling mills and forges, daily and nightly for 12 hours by alternate sets of workpeople. A large proportion of the youths were engaged in long rows of open smith's shops in the production of chains and iron hardware as at Winlaton. As for their moral condition, the ignorance of the boys was deplorable, and instances of total inability to read or write were lamentably frequent.**

The work of a smith's striker is also described, in this case participating in the process of chain making, but the basic principles remain the same whatever particular piece of work is being undertaken.

**Two persons are engaged on each chain. One, an older person, 18 or 20, prepares the iron cut off from a long rod, puts it in the fire, and thence on the shaping anvil, where the 'striker', hammers it into shape. It is then reheated and put on the anvil, where the striker welds it and strikes the flappers that are put over to round it; a cog (or small piece of cast iron) is then put in the middle of the link, to which it is hammered, to prevent the link from drawing together.**

*Right, a souvenir silk programme of the Ascension Day Boat Races of 1850*

# ASCENSION DAY.
# BOAT RACES.

## LIST OF BOATS ENTERED:
### FIRST PRIZE.
## FOR FOUR-OARED BOATS.

FIVE SOVEREIGNS will be given by the Right Worshipful JOSEPH CRAWHALL, ESQ., Mayor of Newcastle, to the First Boat; and ONE SOVEREIGN by RALPH DODDS, ESQ., Sheriff, to the Second Boat.

| NAMES OF BOATS. | OWNERS. | RESIDENCE. | COLOURS. |
|---|---|---|---|
| 1 — SIMON DANSON. | Robert Spoors, | Elswick, | Red and Blue. |
| 2 — WILLIAM TEASDALE, | Thomas Cook, | Dunston, | Red. |
| 3 — ST. AGNES (No. 1.) | Robert Davie, | Close, | Red and White. |
| 4 — FIVE BROTHERS | Robert Clasper, | Derwenthaugh, | Yellow. |
| 5 — INTAKE... | Chairman of the Body of Stewards, | Newcastle, | Green. |

### SECOND PRIZE.
## FOR FOUR-OARED FOY BOATS.

TWO SOVEREIGNS will be given by the MASTER AND BRETHREN of the Trinity House to the First Boat, and ONE SOVEREIGN to the Second Boat.

| | | | |
|---|---|---|---|
| 1 — MAGNET | John Aynsley, | Skinners' Burn, | Blue. |
| 2 — FLATCATCHER, | William Smith, | Dunston, | Blue and White. |
| 3 — FLYING DUTCHMAN, | Selby Brown, | South Shore, | Yellow and Blue. |
| 4 — NUNNYKIRK, | Matthew Brown, | South Shore, | Red and White. |
| 5 — THE ROSE, | William Masters, | Gateshead, | Green. |
| 6 — FIVE BROTHERS | Robert Clasper, | Derwenthaugh, | Yellow. |
| 7 — THE PILOT, | Matthew Taylor, | Ouseburn, | Pink. |
| 8 — GUTTA PERCHA, | George Taylor, | Close, | Crimson. |
| 9 — GREEN FALLOW, | Chairman of the Herbage Committee, | Newcastle, | Pink and Green. |

### THIRD PRIZE.
## FOR TWO OARED BOATS.

TWO SOVEREIGNS will be given by the RIVER COMMITTEE of Newcastle to the First Boat, and ONE SOVEREIGN to the Second Boat.

| | | | |
|---|---|---|---|
| 1 — MAGNET, | James Pratt, | Skinners' Burn, | Blue. |
| 2 — SIMON DANSON, | John Bell, | Elswick, | Red and Blue. |
| 3 — WILLIAM TEASDALE, | Thomas Cook, | Dunston, | Red. |
| 4 — FLYING DUTCHMAN, | Selby Brown, | South Shore, | Yellow and Blue. |
| 5 — NUNNYKIRK, | Matthew Brown, | South Shore, | Red and White. |
| 6 — THE ROSE, | William Masters, | Gateshead, | Green. |
| 7 — THOMAS TROLL, | William Gilpatrick, | Swalwell, | Black. |
| 8 — ST. AGNES, | Nicholas Allan, | Gateshead, | Pink and White. |
| 9 — FIVE BROTHERS, | Richard Clasper, | Derwenthaugh, | Yellow. |
| 10 — THE DUTCHMAN, | Robert Clasper, | Derwenthaugh, | Pink. |

### FOURTH PRIZE.
## A SKIFF RACE.

TWO SOVEREIGNS will be given by the MASTER AND BRETHREN of the Trinity House to the First Skiff, and ONE SOVEREIGN by RALPH DODDS, ESQ., Sheriff, to the Second Skiff.

| | | | |
|---|---|---|---|
| 1 — NEVER SURE, | Thomas Cook, | Dunston, | Red. |
| 2 — MALL TROLL, | William Gilpatrick, | Swalwell, | Black. |
| 3 — COUP DE MAIN, | Henry Clasper, | Newcastle, | Yellow. |
| 4 — FAIRY QUEEN, | James Candlish, | Newcastle, | Blue. |

☞ The Boats Entered for the Prizes are requested to accompany the Barges during the Day.

NOTICE.—The Boats will pass round the North side of the Boat near the Curds and Cream House, and back to the Boat at the High Level Bridge.

*May 6th, 1850.*

Newcastle-upon-Tyne: Printed by M. BENSON, 8, Dean Street.

The older lad, the smith, is the skilled worker of the two; the heating and positioning of the iron is more critical than the swinging of the hammer by the striker. A striker might expect to earn between five and seven shillings for a 72 hour week. If there was a surfeit of work, boys might be kept back for a further 12 hours and then be expected to work their next day shift – a total of 36 hours in one stretch. They were paid overtime, but grindingly hard physical labour over such a long period was bound to have a damaging effect on their health.

Some of the boys, in giving their evidence, tell the inspector what hurts them in carrying out their work. It is easy to see where their bodies were coming under stress. The more robust lads do seem to have been reasonably happy in their work and a strong boy like Renforth may well not have complained but just got stronger, as he became 'trained'. He would have developed considerable upper body strength, which later contributed greatly to his success as a boat rower.

One striker complains that 'the hammer hurts his hands', another, John Watson says, 'Swinging the hammer about, and blowing the bellows makes him bad sometimes; it makes his back work, and his arms, mostly at first, till he got used to it.' (Work = hurt.)

A striker's hammer was not particularly heavy but to swing one all day required considerable stamina. Strikers were not at the bottom of the pile and might expect to go on to become apprenticed as smiths. The boys who carried scrap iron about the works, or performed other completely unskilled tasks were worse paid, worse treated, and, perhaps partly as a consequence, worse behaved.

The Commission also gathered statistics concerning school attendance in Gateshead. Over half the boys aged between five and 15 who lived in Gateshead did not attend school.

It is highly unlikely that that the Renforth children attended school since it would have had to be paid for and the family was poor. James's mother, Jane, was certainly illiterate since she could not sign her name, but made her mark when registering his birth. James was unable to read or write when he embarked on his rowing career, which is why in the early days all sorts of spellings of his name appear in race reports.

James could not have been working in the ironworks for very long when he decided that the life of a soldier would be much more exciting. Although only 13, he twice enlisted in the Army, to be twice promptly retrieved by his father. According to his younger brother John, writing to the *Newcastle Weekly Chronicle* in 1926, their father even had to pay to secure the return of his son. Since James was five years under the legal age of recruitment it seems odd that his father had to buy him out, but perhaps it was a matter of paying back the signing on bounty if young James had already spent it!

The question also arises as to how such a young lad could fool the recruiting sergeant into taking him on. The answer to that is supplied by the political situation of the time. The Crimean War had resulted in heavy casualties in battle and even heavier losses through disease, and those gaps needed to be filled. James was a strapping lad and few awkward questions are asked of promising material at time of war. Renforth senior probably tired of trying to make his headstrong son see the sense in remaining among his own folk in Gateshead, because, a short while later, James had signed up for a third time.

The outbreak of the Indian Mutiny in May 1857 created an urgent need for a fresh batch of recruits, especially since many of the men serving at the end of the Crimean War had already, and controversially, been paid off. James was now just turned 15, and still a long way short of the age limit of 18, nevertheless he joined one of the regiments raised on behalf of the East India Company and was immediately sent off to India.

The voyage took three months, with the recruits doing their basic training on the ship. The fighting continued well into 1858, but lessons learned from the uprising were to lead to political change. On 1st November 1858 a radical restructure of the arrangements for governing India was announced, which resulted in the abolition of the East India Company. Those company soldiers who wished to do so were allowed to return to England. James had by now perhaps decided that Gateshead was not so bad after all, and he would, no doubt, have been missing his family, so he came home. He probably arrived back on Tyneside in 1859 and resumed work as a smith's striker.

Most contemporary accounts, both during James's lifetime and immediately after his death, tell a radically different story about his army service. They say that he joined the Army, 'when he reached his majority' and went to serve in the West Indies, before being bought out by his father. However there is good documentary evidence to show that from age 18 James was resident on Tyneside.

At age 18, on the 23rd July 1860, James joined the Militia, signing on with the Durham Royal Garrison Artillery in Gateshead. The signing on Bounty, and the two pence a day more than the infantry that Artillery recruits received, would no doubt have been welcome. Records held at the Public Records Office, Kew, show Renforth to have been present at all the annual musters of the Durham Royal Garrison Artillery from 1860 to 1869. At this time the Militia were not required to serve overseas, which places James firmly in England, not in the Regular Army, and not in the West Indies. He married Mary Ann Bell at Newcastle Register Office on the 26th June 1861, when both their addresses are given as Concord Court, Newcastle. As one would expect, James's occupation at the time was as a smith's striker, but rather strangely his age is recorded as 23 years, when really he was only 19. Maybe he had just got used to adding four years to his real age after lying his way into military service with the East India Company. It is difficult to speculate as to why the alternative story of military service in the West Indies arose. Whatever the reason it is clear that, after he returned from India, James remained on Tyneside until his Canadian adventures in 1870 and 1871.

It is possible to trace something of James's life during the first few years of the 1860s through the registrations of the births of two daughters and the death of one of them. On 29th June 1862, Mary gave birth to their first daughter, Margaret

*The rundown Tuthill Stairs, c.1879, where Renforth's first daughter died in 1863. A poster advertises the Tyne Regatta.*

Jane, at Dean Court, Newcastle. Sadly, only seven months later, on 21st January 1863, Margaret Jane died of bronchitis at Tuthill Stairs, Newcastle, just up from the Quayside. Although this was a blow for the Renforths, infant death was common in Victorian times and many families would have experienced the death of a child. James and Mary probably accepted their baby's death as being unfortunate but not unusual. In any case Mary was soon pregnant again, giving birth to Ann Elizabeth, in the Lying in Hospital, New Bridge Street, Newcastle on 21st December 1863. James's occupation is recorded in the register as 'Iron Foundry Striker' and the family were by then living at Bailiff Gate, Newcastle.

James Renforth found himself with a hard, dirty, poorly paid job, and a wife and child to support. He had been a good swimmer from his early years: Victorian photographs show 'mudlarks' enjoying a swim in the Tyne, and the Renforth family lived in an ideal spot for their boys to play in the river. His brother John says that James was such a good swimmer as a boy, he was nicknamed 'The Dolphin'. James saw that his great stamina and strength, coupled with his undoubted ability in the water, might enable him to earn extra money. His younger brother Stephen was also an excellent swimmer. Renforth's first outing was in a handicap race at the Northumberland Baths, Newcastle, and he succeeded in winning a beautiful gold medal which he prized for the rest of his life. He next competed in a handicap race in the Tyne opposite the (King's) Meadows island, winning another handsome medal provided by the promoters of the contest, the Newcastle Swimming Club. Renforth then lost in Durham and at Tynemouth to the renowned swimmer Thomas Pape of Newcastle – the race at Tynemouth culminating in a thrilling finish. Renforth had put in some hard training after his defeat in Durham and this time he was very close to beating his rival.

At some point he competed in a swimming race at Talkin Tarn, and although he did not win, it became the subject of an anecdote which was repeated later in his rowing career to illustrate what a determined character he was. The story relates to a time when he was desperately short of money. Lacking the means to pay his fare to Talkin Tarn sports, where there was a prize of a few pounds to be contended for by swimmers, Renforth set out on foot. Talkin Tarn, near Carlisle, is over 50 miles from Newcastle, but Renforth, undaunted by the distance, walked nearly all night to reach the place. Unsurprisingly after such an effort he failed to win the race and presumably, since he would still be out of funds, he then had to turn round and walk back again! His fierce determination was a great strength but it was also a potential weakness. In this case walking all night left him in no condition to win the prize: he would have been better off staying at home.

Renforth's desire to make something of himself was as strong as ever but swimming did not provide big enough prizes, and the season was short, with most races taking place outdoors. A change of job may have turned his attention to boat rowing as a possible route to success.

In 1866 James was employed to ferry men and materials by boat on the Tyne as part of the work to demolish the Tyne Bridge. Rowing every day as part of his job he perhaps realised that he had the talent to make it as a professional oarsman and looked at ways to develop his career in that direction.

# Early Days 1866-67

I t appears that being part of the workforce engaged in the demolition of the Tyne
Bridge was quite significant in Renforth's life, and in the development of his rowing
career. Much later, when he had become a heroic figure on Tyneside, a group of his
former workmates from the bridge demolition were to carry his coffin from Gateshead
railway station to a hearse waiting to take the body to his James Street home. But in
1866 he was just one of the lads, enjoying the freedom and fresh air of working on the
river instead of hammering metal in a hot and dirty foundry.

The 1781 bridge, which was of stone construction and consisted of nine arches,
was being removed to allow further industrial development upriver. The low arches pre-
vented colliers and other sea going vessels from travelling upstream of the bridge to
load and discharge their cargoes. On the Newcastle bank the Elswick works of W.G.
Armstrong were rapidly expanding and needed to export their products by sea but were
unable to do so until a bridge could be built which allowed the passage of large vessels.
The replacement bridge would be the now much loved Swing Bridge but that was not
completed until 1876 and forms no part of our story.

*Tyne & Wear Archives*

*This picture was taken for the Tyne Improvement Commission in 1865, just before demolition of
the old bridge began.*

Each day that he rowed the demolition men back and forth to the old Tyne Bridge helped to increase Renforth's strength, and his skill as a waterman. We do not know if he was spotted as a likely talent by the Boyd brothers, members of a Gateshead rowing family, or if he approached the Boyds for assistance with training to become a rower, but they seem to have been handling him in these very early stages of his career. Renforth quickly picked up the rudiments of rowing in open boats and had his first professional race not long after starting work on the Tyne Bridge demolition.

While he was still best known as a swimmer, it was probably in the early months of 1866 that he had his first contest on the Tyne as a rower, competing for money, against a youth named Robinson, who also boasted an alias, 'Princey'! Alas, 'Princey's' royal pretensions were misplaced since after taking an early lead he 'blew up' allowing Renforth to win quite comfortably, but we know little of the match, and a later *Chronicle* biographical sketch of Renforth does not mention the race at all.

Renforth's next match was against G. Curry of Gateshead, rowed on the evening of Saturday 19th May 1866 from the High Level Bridge to the Meadows public house, a distance of about two miles for a stake of £20. Renforth was the favourite at the start, and the tone of the short account in the following Monday's *Chronicle* suggests that even at this early stage he was being viewed as a useful prospect. The competitors rowed in Harry Clasper's fine open boats with both men being regarded as novices. Renforth had a reputation as a swimmer but little was known of his ability on the water. Curry was a small man, weighing just $8^{1/2}$ stone (119 lbs), while Renforth was something like $2^{1/2}$ stones heavier, at 11 stone (154 lbs). The size difference was bound to act to his benefit if he could pull his weight. Accordingly the odds were on Renforth at five to four, that is to place a bet on Renforth you had to risk £5 to gain £4 from a supporter of Curry. Renforth won the toss and chose the northern, inside, station, which, all other things being equal, is favoured on the Tyne course, with the Annie and King's Meadows islands coming into play before the $1^{1/2}$ mile mark (see map, page 20).

At the start Curry got away much the better of the two and after only a few hundred yards showed a length in front. By the time the pair had reached Skinner's Burn, about 600 yards into the race, Curry was able to take Renforth's water and the odds had switched round to 5 to 4 on Curry. Renforth did not give up and, sticking to his task, he gradually crept close to his opponent so that at the Shot Tower they were almost level again. Renforth's greater strength now began to tell and, despite Curry's game efforts, Renforth was clear at Clasper's boat house and the race was effectively over, Renforth passing the Meadows public house, the Countess of Coventry, 50 yards ahead of his opponent.

Renforth now sought a new opponent and his challenge, published in the

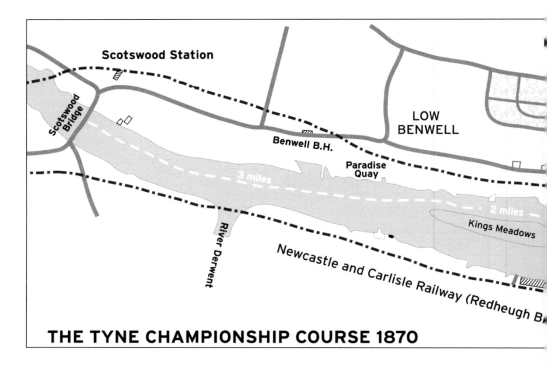

## THE TYNE CHAMPIONSHIP COURSE 1870

*Newcastle Daily Chronicle* of Saturday June 23rd 1866, shows that he did not have a particular sculler in mind. Any one of the young oarsmen from the south side of the river would do, although his careful handicapping demands indicate that he was not yet confident in his powers as a sculler.

> JAMES RANFORD, of Gateshead, will row any of the following men for £10 aside. He will take two lengths of Makepeace, of Gateshead; or will row young Smith, of Dunston, level; or will take one length of Robson, of the Windmill Hills, Gateshead, in H. Clasper's outrigger boats. Any of these matches can be made at T. Jackson's, Blue Bell, Gateshead, between eight and ten on Saturday night.

This challenge came to nothing and Renforth did not row competitively again in 1866, but continued to train both for swimming and for rowing. For the moment his career as a professional oarsman had stalled and he must have doubted whether he would ever get a chance to make a name for himself.

The 1867 rowing season began with the *Chronicle* of March 27th analysing prospects for the coming year, an analysis which made no mention of Renforth. Clearly

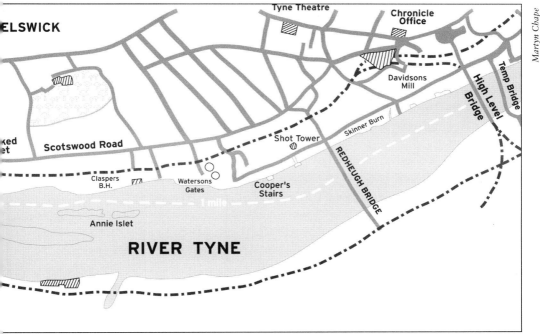

Map showing ELSWICK, Tyne Theatre, Chronicle Office, Davidsons Mill, Scotswood Road, Shot Tower, Skinner Burn, Claspers B.H., Watersons Gates, Cooper's Stairs, REDHEUGH BRIDGE, High Level Bridge, Temp Bridge, Annie Islet, RIVER TYNE. *Martyn Chape*

he was not regarded as important enough for inclusion. However in April 1867 Renforth rowed his next race, against Bambrough, another Gateshead man, in a race over a mile. The *Chronicle* report was short and to the point, neither man being well-known.

**BOAT RACE ON THE TYNE FOR £20.** – Yesterday afternoon, W. Bambrough and J. Ranford, of Gateshead, met on the Tyne at the High Level Bridge, to decide their sculling powers, to row to Waterston's Gates – one mile – In Percy's open skiffs. The Anthony Nicol steamer attended; Mr. W. Matfin being the referee. Ranford was the favourite at something like 2 to 1, and certainly the race justified the odds, for from the start to the finish Bambrough never had a squeak. Ranford lost his choice of sides, consequently he had to take the south side, but it had no effect in reference to his chance, for when they reached the Skinner Burn about three lengths separated them, and at the finish Ranford was nearly double that distance in advance, and won with the greatest of ease.

*Newcastle Daily Chronicle* Tuesday April 23rd 1867

Following this victory Renforth tried to secure another match and a challenge appeared in the *Newcastle Daily Chronicle* of Monday June 3rd 1867:

**JAMES RENFORD** will row Wm Hornsby, best and best boats from High Level Bridge to Meadows House, on June 22nd. A match can be made at Mr Jackson's, Blue Bell, Gateshead, on Monday night, June 3rd, between 8 and 9.

This match did not take place and it may be that at this stage of his career Renforth had little influence among Tyneside's sporting gentlemen and thus lacked the connections to turn challenges into races. The Blue Bell was not a major sporting house, nor was Mr Jackson a significant figure on the rowing scene. But things were about to change

Renforth's impressive private trials came to the notice of George Brown, the land-lord of the Battery Inn, Forth Street, Newcastle, and Mr Stewart of Stewart and Young, plumbers, gas fitters and brass founders, of Market Street, Newcastle. They took a great interest in the young man, quickly becoming his principal backers and offering him every facility at the Battery Inn, which became his training quarters. Renforth won a heat in an open boat handicap race at Talkin Tarn Regatta, near Carlisle, and then, in mid-August, he was matched with the Boyd brothers in two contests which were to prove significant in his quest for success as an oarsman. His association with Brown and Stewart allowed him to race for a much higher stake than he had been able to raise previously, and, since the two businessmen had wooed him away from his Gateshead companions, it is not surprising that the races against the brothers, particularly that

*Detail from a watercolour by Wilson Hepple of King's Meadows island with the Countess of Coventry pub, a coxed four and wherry.*

*The start of a skiff race on the Tyne. The heavily industrialised Gateshead bank of the river forms the backdrop while, beneath the High Level Bridge, the spectator boats prepare to follow the race.*

against Robert, were something of a grudge match.

The arrangements were made at the Star Hotel, Northumberland Street, Newcastle, and to a casual observer it might have seemed that Renforth had bitten off more than he could chew. He had agreed to race in open boats for £50 against the younger Boyd, Robert, on the 21st September, and then in skiffs for £100 against Robert's older brother, James, on the 5th October. The match against Robert being over a $1^{3/4}$ mile course, High Level Bridge to the Meadows House, and against James being over a $3^{1/2}$ mile course, High Level Bridge to Scotswood Bridge. The race in skiffs would be Renforth's first contest in this type of boat and James Boyd, although now 36 years old, was known to be a fine sculler.

The majority of contests on the Tyne took place in either the sort of open boats used by Robert Boyd and Renforth or in the skiffs used for the race with James Boyd so this is probably a good place to give a description of the two types of craft. Both types were also known as 'wager' boats, boats in which races were rowed with money being staked on the result.

Races in open boats usually, although not always, were contested in specified matched craft from one of the boathouses on the Tyne. In this case the boats were from James Hall's boathouse and were the matched boats *Lily* and *Rose*. Anybody could hire the boats to race for a bet, and, since they were as near identical as possible, the contest would hinge entirely on the skill, strength and endurance of the participants. The other advantage this sort of contest had for the novice rower was that he did not need to have a boat of his own. The *Newcastle Daily Chronicle* of Tuesday May 3rd 1870 gives a detailed description of James Hall's most well-known pair of open boats, *G* and *H*.

> **Five streak craft, weighing 79lbs each, built on the same lines, and fitted in every respect similar. Their dimensions are as follows:-**
>
> | | |
> |---|---|
> | Length | 20 ft |
> | Extreme breadth | 24 ins |
> | Height forward | $12^{3}/_{4}$ ins |
> | Height aft | 12 ins |
> | Height amidships | $9^{1}/_{2}$ ins |
>
> **G is a pound heavier than H.**

Open boats were fitted with iron outriggers and had fixed seats. Contestants tossed a coin to decide who would have choice of boat. In public contests the articles of agreement often specified that the boats should not be customised in any way and that an inspection should be made by the owner of the boats immediately prior to the race to ensure that things were exactly as they should be and that no alterations had been made.

Skiffs were longer and much more lightly built than open boats and were the Formula 1 craft of the rowing scene. Considerable skill was required just to stay upright, and the shallowness of the boats required them to be decked, with a cockpit in which the sculler sat. Harry Clasper must take much of the credit for developing this sort of craft on the Tyne. In November 1868, when challenging for the championship of England, Renforth used the skiff *Alderman Cowen M.P.*

This skiff was made of cedar by Robert Jewitt of Dunston, and was of the following dimensions:

| | |
|---|---|
| Length | 30 ft |
| Width amidships | $11^{3}/_{4}$ ins |
| Height at stem | $3^{3}/_{4}$ ins |
| Height at stern | $2^{7}/_{8}$ ins |
| Weight | 30 lbs. |

Skiffs were also fitted with iron outriggers and had fixed seats. Articles of agreement often specified that matches were to be rowed in 'best and best boats', which meant the best boat that each contestant could obtain for the race. Skiff races were a test of man and craft, although boats were frequently supplied by the same builder and were very similar in design and construction.

While in training for his forthcoming matches, Renforth continued to take part in swimming contests. He beat Edward Boddy at a Newcastle Swimming Club competition in the Tyne, and won a medal for his efforts, only a month before he was due to row his open boat race against Robert Boyd.

Renforth, although still a novice – the *Newcastle Daily Journal* of 23rd September 1867 in its preamble to an account of the race reported, ' ... Neither man can boast of even any second rate achievement' – was favourite for the contest with the younger Boyd. Boyd, at 32, was well-built but did not use his strength to good effect when sculling, and Renforth, who was described as 'strongly built', had made sufficient impression on the followers of aquatics for odds of 3 and 4 to 1 to be offered on him without finding any takers.

The race took place at 8am on the morning of Saturday 21st September 1867, and despite the early start there was a good crowd of spectators. As with all races which take place in tidal waters, timing of the start was dependent on the lunar cycle. It was usual on the Tyne to start races one hour before high tide. This allowed contestants to race up river with the last of the flood tide. Boyd put off from the Gateshead side in his choice of boat, *Lily*, and was soon joined by Renforth, who put off from the Mansion House on the Newcastle bank in *Rose*. Boyd won the toss for choice of station and opted for the northern side. When they took up position beneath the second arch of the High Level Bridge both men were cheered, and given advice, as is the way with crowds!

Renforth was quickest away and in less than thirty yards was three-quarters of a length ahead, but Boyd quickly fought back and by the time they had reached Davidson's Mill was on even terms. Encouraged by their man's rally, backers of Boyd now found that nobody was prepared to take them on! Renforth soon forced his way back into the lead, but in his inexperience risked a foul by steering too far to the north, but Boyd was not tactically astute and was unable to take advantage. Renforth continued to make progress and legitimately took Boyd's water at the Skinner Burn. Boyd was beaten even at this early stage and the final mile and a half became a procession, with 100 to 1 offered against Boyd at Clasper's Boat House, and Renforth winning as he pleased by six lengths. Renforth's bad feeling against Boyd clearly had not been assuaged by his victory since he failed to make a collection on behalf of his opponent, which behaviour the *Journal* described in its understated way as 'ungenerous'.

The race had been won in the first quarter of a mile and gave only a very limited guide to the true abilities of the winner. The contest with the elder Boyd which was to take place a fortnight later would be a much sterner test for the up and coming Renforth.

At 7.45am on the morning of Saturday 5th October 1867 Renforth and James Boyd put off in skiffs to race from the High Level Bridge to the Scotswood Suspension Bridge, a distance of $3^{1}/_{2}$ miles. Betting was 6 to 4 on Renforth but few wagers were made and most of the gambling activity took place aboard the official steamer, the *Mystery,* which was following the race. On the Friday night Renforth had won the toss for the choice of station and he elected to start on the north, Newcastle, side. The water was calm and the tide was running only sluggishly as the flood began to slacken. They were allowed ten minutes to start by mutual agreement and if they failed to get away in that time they were to be started by pistol shot. At 7.55 they appeared beneath the second arch of the bridge. Renforth now stripped to the waist, but Boyd remained in his flannels. As they waited at the start there was a flurry of betting activity. Renforth positioned himself too close to his opponent, and almost caused a foul at the start, before his backers urged him to move further to the north.

Both men got a clean start, without the pistol being required, and after 50 yards Boyd showed three feet in the lead, but Renforth fought back and was level at the Mansion House. Boyd spurted again and forced his skiff back in front, with Renforth remaining close and getting on terms before the Skinner's Burn had been reached, where Boyd began to feel the pressure. Renforth now showed in the lead and Boyd was forced to steer further to the south to avoid fouling. At the Shot Tower Renforth was two lengths in front and before the mile had been reached it was evident that Renforth had control of the contest. At the mile and three-quarter mark Renforth held a five length lead and he won as he pleased, by seven lengths in 25 minutes 40 seconds. Either Renforth had brushed up his rowing etiquette or he liked James better than his younger brother because he duly made a collection after the race for the loser, who took his defeat in good part. Both statements may be true since by November Renforth and James Boyd were training together on the water.

Renforth's rowing style came in for some comment in the *Journal*'s report of this race and it is clear that his distinctive technique had already developed to the extent that it was readily contrasted with that of the old Tyne champion, Bob Chambers. While Chambers was renowned for his long, powerful stroke, the *Journal* concedes that the 'lively, interesting, stroke, which is nothing short of a puzzle to understand' used by Renforth propelled his skiff with unusual ease. Renforth was already sliding on his seat, making use of the footboard and utilising his thigh muscles to row a rapid but powerful sweeping stroke. It was not as pretty as the long stroke of practised watermen

*An enthusiastic crowd on Scotswood Bridge greets the contestants at the end of a skiff race on the Tyne.*

like Chambers or Harry Kelley, the current English champion, but it was extraordinarily effective.

Renforth's victory took little out of him and he was in his boat, training on the river, the very next day while his backers looked round for another opponent. No time was wasted in arranging a skiff race for a stake of £100 against John Bright, who was reckoned to be one of the finest exponents of open boat rowing on the Tyne and was also highly regarded as a skiff rower. Bright, who came from the Mushroom, Newcastle, was three years younger than Renforth but had rowed his first race when barely in his teens and had competed successfully on the Tyne since 1864. Bright's first job had been as a potter but he was attracted to life on the river and when offered a career as a waterman he swiftly made the change. The race was due to take place on the 9th December and by the 11th November both men were in training and had taken delivery of new boats built especially for the contest. Renforth's boat was built by Jewitt of Dunston and Bright's was built by James Hall.

Early in December both men were in hard training. Renforth was a slight favourite at 5 to 4 on, but a close race was being eagerly awaited. But it was not to be. Bright had been troubled with a cold in early November, which had interrupted his training, and he was struck down again with a cold immediately before the race. He was forced to withdraw and had to forfeit the £40 which had been put down.

It is probably worth explaining how the finances of the race stakes worked. Money was deposited with the stakeholder, usually a sporting publican, before the race. In the case of a contest for a small amount it would be put down, or 'planked', the night before the race. Bigger stakes were paid over in a much more complex and structured manner and the stakeholder might be a newspaper with a sporting readership. On Tyneside the stakeholder for big races was frequently the *Newcastle Daily Chronicle* and in London it was usually *Bell's Life*. When a challenge was first made, often in licensed premises, the two parties involved, sometimes backers, but it might be the rowers themselves, especially if they were of some standing, would put down perhaps a sovereign each as 'binding' money. Then if they woke up the next morning with a sore head and the realisation that they had made an unwise match they only lost that sovereign! Sometimes both parties would wake up, each with a sore head, realise that for practical reasons the match could not be continued with, and agree to take back their money. And then sometimes there was a dispute, with claims for money to be forfeited being denied by the party who no longer wished to go on with the contest. A troublesome opponent would be told that unless he behaved properly he would never be offered a race again.

Once the rowers were bound, at least morally and by the sovereign, articles of agreement were drawn up and signed by the protagonists or their nominees and witnessed. The articles, which were in effect legally binding contracts, specified how the stakes were to be paid over as well as providing full details of the course, the time of the race, and the rules under which it was to take place. Typically there would be four or five payments, made at different public houses on a Friday night, no doubt to spread the trade around the backers' businesses, culminating in a final payment the night before the race. Thus, if as in the case of John Bright, a rower became ill a few days before a match, 80 per cent of the stake had already been paid to the stakeholder, and that money was forfeited to the opponent and his backers.

The cancellation of the match with Bright left Renforth fully trained but without an opponent. Another Newcastle sculler of considerable reputation, and a member of the champion four, who was to have a considerable influence on the rest of Renforth's career, now offered a contest. James Taylor challenged Renforth to row a skiff race from the High Level Bridge to the Meadows House ($1^3/_4$ miles) for £50, the race to take place within a fortnight, that is before Christmas. This would have been another big step up in class for Renforth, and he and his backers sought more time for him to prepare. On December 14th 1867 at the Star Hotel, Northumberland Street, Newcastle, they offered Taylor a race in March 1868 but he declined. Bright was also present and was keen to set up a race with Renforth in open boats, the craft in which Bright was most confident, but no agreement could be reached. Renforth's reputation as a powerful sculler was beginning to get around and his chances of securing races were probably not helped by his backer Mr Stewart's boast, made at around this time, that Renforth could give any man two lengths start and still win. Professional rowing was all about money, and rowers and their backers did not wish to take part in races which they thought they were bound to lose.

As 1867 drew to a close Renforth tested himself on land with a bowling contest against John King over a mile on Newcastle's Town Moor for a £4 stake. The rules were simple – the winner was the first man to get his 25 oz bowl past the mile post. Inevitably there was gambling; King was favourite at 7 to 4 on, and indeed King took the lead in the first throw and won by half a throw. Two days later, on Christmas Day, Renforth was back on the water taking part in a scratch pair oar contest in James Hall's open boats, rowing with George Hawkins. They won their trial heat, half a mile with the tide, but lost the next race to the eventual winners, R. Armstrong and C. Hutchinson.

1867 had been a good year for James Renforth. He had linked up with two influential backers and both in his training and in his races had shown himself to have great potential as a boat rower. He had made these advances without anything that could be called proper coaching and it appeared to many observers that there was more improvement to come. The approaching year would show that the extent of that advance was beyond the dreams of the most ardent of James Renforth's supporters.

## JAMES HALL,

### *BOAT BUILDER,*

## TYNESIDE TERRACE, NEWCASTLE,

*Adjoining the Tyne Amateur Rowing Club Boat House,*

Skiffs of all kinds, with latest improvements. speedily built.

Estimates on application.

# ... a good class 'dark' man ...

The *Newcastle Daily Chronicle* printed a review of the Aquatic Year (1867) on January 4th 1868, in which they charted Renforth's progress as a sculler, from being a rumour of 'a good class "dark" man' before his races with the Boyds, to fully-fledged aquatic prospect who experienced oarsmen were sidestepping by the end of the year. In order to overcome the problem of Tyneside's scullers running scared, Renforth's first act of the the New Year had been to send a challenge to some of the Thames men, published in *The Sportsman* of January 2nd 1868.

**James Randford, of Gateshead, is willing to row Coombes, Edwards, Pedgrift, or Kilsby, of London, for £50 a-side, and give or take £10 expenses to row on the Thames or the Tyne. An answer through the medium of** *The Sportsman* **will be attended to.**

It should be understood that Renforth, an illiterate smith's striker from Gateshead, was not acting alone in throwing out challenges through the London Press. Messrs Brown and Stewart were providing advice and material support to their protégé, not purely through philanthropic feelings for the young man, but as an investment. They were hoping to win money by backing Renforth, and in the case of George Brown it was also good for trade at the Battery Inn. And not only were they supporters of James Renforth, they now took his younger brother Stephen into the stable as well. A match had been made on the 4th January between Stephen Renforth and William Harrison, alias 'The Ratcatcher' to row a skiff race from the High Level Bridge to the Meadows House ($1^{3}/_{4}$ miles), on the 25th January, for a stake of £10. Stephen was to stay at the Battery Inn during his preparation for the contest and was to be trained by his brother James.

Something was amiss however, since on Friday 24th January the Renforths forfeited their binding sovereign and the match was ended. Two weeks later James Renforth issued a challenge through the *Newcastle Daily Chronicle* offering to row a skiff race for £50 on either the Thames or Tyne championship courses against Tom Wise of London or Mark Addy of Manchester. Tellingly he gave his contact address as the Tiger Inn, Pilgrim Street, Newcastle, signalling that a rift had opened up between Renforth and George Brown. James was no longer able to use the Battery Inn as his training headquarters.

The break up was confirmed when John Bright challenged James to a race in Clasper's open boats for £25 a-side and suggested that they met on February 29th at Baird's house, the Star Hotel, Northumberland Street, Newcastle, to sign articles of agreement. Renforth went to the Star, but after a good deal of banter admitted that he had fallen out with his backers and could only raise a stake of £10. Bright felt that to row for a total of £20 would barely cover his expenses and would not race for less than £15 a-side. No agreement could be reached until at 10.30pm Bright, perhaps feeling more mellow by then, agreed to row in James Hall's open boats for £10 a-side and articles were signed for a race on the 28th March. There was general satisfaction among followers of the sport that the two were going to race at last.

This was a difficult time for James Renforth. His backers for the forthcoming race were ordinary working men who had scraped together the stake money and there were no businessmen to support him during the training period. James Hall of the Elswick Boathouse acted as umpire for him during the race with Bright so perhaps Renforth was afforded some help in kind during the build up to the match but there was no longer an avuncular publican to minister to his needs. Unless he could find other backers his career would come to a halt, because to row against the best he would need considerable sums for his share of the stake. He had been lucky that John Bright, in a spirit of friendly rivalry, had agreed to race for just £20.

After making five deposits of £2 each during the build up, both men were fit and well as they prepared to race on the afternoon of Saturday 28th March 1868. The race was due off soon after 6pm, an ideal time to gather a big crowd of spectators.

The High Level Bridge was packed with people, including groups of men clinging to unlikely and vertiginous vantage points. Even the temporary Tyne Bridge, which was downstream of the course, was crowded. Thousands of spectators lined the river banks and the four steamers which were to follow the race were perilously overloaded. Renforth won the toss for choice of the matched boats, and selected H, while Bright rowed in G. Renforth also won the toss for sides and took the favoured northern station. The setting sun cast a warm glow over the calm waters of the River Tyne – perfect conditions for a boat race. Betting, which up to now had been sluggish, suddenly became brisk, mostly at even money. Friends of Renforth occasionally called out for 5 to 4 against their man, but very few supporters of Bright accepted those odds.

The men stripped, climbed into their boats, and went through their warm-up routines on the river. Observers felt that Renforth looked rather fleshy, and when in his preliminaries he rowed at a tremendous pace there was speculation that he would not last the race. Five attempts were made to start before finally the cry, 'They're off' signalled that the contest was under way.

Bright took the lead about 50 yards from the start and after 200 yards was a quarter of a length in front. Renforth now got seriously to work and at the Skinner's Burn, around 600 yards, with Renforth settling well to his own sweeping stroke, he crept into the lead. Bright stuck to his man but Renforth pulled out a lead of half a length. Odds of 5 to 4 on Renforth were offered, and accepted, by the supporters of Bright who expected their man to get his second wind. The two sets of spectators encouraged their men with cries of 'Gan on Jack' and 'Gan on Jim', but Renforth had established a lead of three lengths at the Shot Tower (1,100 yards) and continued to control the race despite huge efforts from Bright to force his way back into contention. Renforth won by six lengths in 13 minutes 22 seconds, looking fresh, while his opponent finished in a distressed state. He collected 33 shillings for the loser aboard the referee's boat and then rowed back to James Hall's Elswick Boathouse where he was loudly cheered.

In conclusion to its report of the race, the *Newcastle Daily Chronicle* of Monday 30th March 1868, although excited by the prospect of finding a worthy successor to Harry Clasper and Bob Chambers, sounded a note of caution:

**The victor in this race may now be said to be starting upon a new career, and he will do well to remember as he goes along his way that besides immense stamina and undeniably first-class rowing there are other qualities which it is necessary for an oarsman to possess before he can fairly and honourably reach the summit of the rowing art, the goal of all his wishes. He must be steady and docile in his training, straightforward in all his relations with his backers, and intelligent as well as muscular in the boat and out of it. It is years since so promising a young sculler was seen on Tyneside, and it is to be hoped he will so conduct himself as to bring credit and honour to his native place.**

Upstart young scullers probably did not need to be reminded of their place. However successful a Clasper, a Chambers, or even a Renforth, might become they retained their lowly social status and at least knew that they should mind their Ps and Qs when dealing with their betters, even if they sometimes found it difficult! Leaving that aside, Renforth's position had been improved considerably by his victory over Bright. He still required influential, and wealthy, backers, but he was the newest and brightest aquatic star in the Tyneside firmament and looked a good investment for any sporting gentleman.

Renforth was immensely strong and had a tremendously impressive physique. Five feet $7^{1/2}$ inches tall, which was a bit above average for the time, he was very thickset, and on more than one occasion it was remarked that because he was so powerfully

*Renforth in 1871. He gazes impassively at the camera in this 'rustic' studio portrait.*

built he appeared shorter than his measured height. He measured 42 inches around the chest which gave him plenty of scope for making full use of his lungs in a tough match. For his races Renforth usually weighed in at a few pounds over 11 stone, and although today, especially in rowing circles, he would be regarded as a lightweight, in his own time he was reckoned a heavyweight. Indeed in the first contest of which we have a record of the weights, his opponent, Curry, only weighed $8^{1}/_{2}$ stone. Renforth, as the 'big un,' was a hot favourite, and, winning easily, amply justified his favouritism. When he was not in hard training his weight would quickly increase and there are many, many reports of him being 'quite gross', 'big in condition', or looking 'very big'. Potential opponents soon tried to exploit this tendency for his weight to balloon by challenging him to race at short notice in the hope that Renforth would take them on while still above his best rowing weight. He suffered from regular but probably fairly infrequent epileptic fits, usually it seems when he was excited and also when he had taken alcoholic drink. His epilepsy does not appear to have had a deleterious effect on his rowing career but as will become clear it may well have been a significant factor in his sudden death.

He is described as being dark complexioned and photographs taken in 1871 show him with short dark hair parted in the centre and sporting a goatee beard. He looks neither happy nor sad but there is a hint of determination behind his impassive gaze. In one of the photographs he is wearing a light coloured suit with a waistcoat, watch and chain, and does indeed give the impression of being quite short. As with many athletes, clothes seem to hang awkwardly from his heavily muscled limbs and in particular his massive thighs cause the cloth to bulge when he is sitting down.

A description of Renforth in the *South Durham Herald* for Saturday July 17th 1869, when he appeared at the Hartlepools Regatta of 1869, gives a good impression of how he looked when stripped to race:

> **… and when he stepped into the skiff preparatory to the contest in which he was engaged, a buzz of admiration greeted the sight of his gigantic biceps, on the ropy and swelling surface of which was a tattooed design of a striking character.**

His tattooed arms are mentioned on one another occasion but it seems that the 'design of a striking character' must remain a mystery. An engraving of Renforth in a skiff on the Tyne, stripped to the waist as was customary, shows no tattoos at all.

For the moment Renforth began to spread his wings within the local rowing scene – stroking a four-oar in the 'Jolly Dogs' handicap but losing in the final – and trying to get a match off the ground with James Taylor.

James Taylor, who was a wherryman and a member of the famous rowing and boatbuilding Taylor family, was a clever sculler but a few pounds too light to compete successfully against the best of the bigger men. However a study of his behaviour during pre-match manouvering shows him to be without equal at getting under his opponents' skin, and in arranging contests at times and under conditions which best suited him. James Taylor had put out a challenge to race anybody but the ex-champion, Bob Chambers, for £50 a-side and Renforth tried to take him up on his offer.

Renforth had a bit of a problem however in that he was a member of the Militia and had to go and do his annual training of 27 days with the Durham Royal Garrison Artillery in a fortnight's time. Taylor, not unreasonably on this occasion, felt that Renforth was already fit from training for his race with Bright, while he would be at a disadvantage if he had to race at such short notice. Despite two meetings to try and and set up a match the two parties could not come to an agreement and the matter was

*Robert Chambers in his rowing cos-tume, probably in 1859.*

shelved at least until Renforth had returned from his annual camp. Since Renforth was contemplating a match where his share of the stake was £50, when only a few weeks previously he had been unable to raise £15, it appears that things must have been looking up as far as backers were concerned. Sure enough the *Newcastle Daily Chronicle* of Monday April 13th 1868 reported:

> **… that Randford and his two principal supporters – Mr. Stewart and Mr. George Brown, of the Battery Inn, Newcastle – have at length settled all their grievances, and are now as friendly as could be wished.**

Renforth now tried hard, no doubt with the active assistance of Messrs Brown and Stewart, to bring off a £50 a-side race with Joseph Heath of Wandsworth, who had expressed an interest in taking on the Gateshead man. This also fell through when Heath declined to race – perhaps he had been warned during these preliminaries that Renforth was a real 'tartar'. Renforth returned from his army training and resumed his efforts to rise through the boat rowing ranks. He was a member of the Northern

Rowing Club, one of the two major professional rowing clubs on the Tyne, the other being the Albion Rowing Club. Towards the end of May a new professional four-oared crew was formed from Northern members with a view to taking part in the forthcoming local regattas. It consisted of Thomas Matfin (stroke), James Renforth, Thomas Winship and William Matfin. The current Champion Four was made up of members of the Albion Club, Robert Chambers (ex-champion), Andrew Thompson, Matthew Scott, and James Taylor. However Robert Chambers was once again in the grip of tuberculosis and a replacement would probably need to be found for the coming season. On the 4th June 1868, after a long struggle, with every journey to Darlington or Morpeth to obtain a change of air recorded in the local press, 'Honest' Bob Chambers gave up the fight for life.

For the moment the Tyneside rowing fraternity were united in sadness at the death of Robert Chambers. Renforth attended the funeral on the 7th June and is listed in the newspaper report of the occasion as an 'immediate friend', perhaps a sign of his rising status. As becomes clear later, Chambers was a Freemason and Renforth certainly became one at some stage, so it is possible that the Freemasonry connection also helped to propel him into the ranks of the immediate friends among the mourners.

A rumour now began to circulate, and was published in the *Newcastle Daily Journal* of 8th June 1868, that Renforth had challenged the champion Kelley, and that Kelley had declined the proposal. Renforth's backers issued a denial in the *Newcastle Daily Chronicle* of the 9th June and insisted that the challenge had been meant for Heath, and that Kelley was kindly helping them out by passing on Renforth's challenge to any second-rate waterman he might know. In fact what seems to have happened was that a number of the mourners at Chambers's funeral adjourned to a pub for a drink afterwards, and Mr Stewart, who seems not to have been the most tactful of men, had offered Kelley £10 expenses to row against Renforth on the Tyne. Kelley had replied jokily, saying that Renforth's looks were quite good enough for him thank you, and he must decline. Obviously Kelley could see that Renforth had potential, but at this stage there was no serious attempt to match the two. Since Heath had declined to race, Renforth was still looking for a suitable opponent for a sculling match. He was entered for the sculling races at various regattas through the summer, but the real money was to be made by competing in matches for high stakes.

In the meantime there was a promise of some four-oar action against the Champion crew, who had brought Robert Chambers's (deceased, ex-champion) namesake, Robert Chambers (Wallsend) in as a replacement for 'Honest' Bob. There was a proposal to have a race between the Northern and the Champion, Albion, crews for a few pounds, in order to decide who should represent the Tyne in the upcoming regattas. This would save on the expense of sending two Tyne crews around the country, when inevitably only the better of the two could come back with the prize. This proposal was reported in the *Newcastle Daily Chronicle* of 15th June 1868, but also expressed in the article was a concern that the arrangements for the match might be delayed because Renforth had suffered a sudden illness at Tynemouth on the previous day. One wonders if this sudden illness was an epileptic fit since the paper was suggesting that the match might be set up only 24 hours after he was taken ill. It was unlikely to have been an infection, since in these pre-antibiotic days bacterial infections normally required a considerable time for recovery.

The following Saturday Thomas Matfin went to the Trafalgar Inn, New Bridge Street, Newcastle, the house of James Taylor, and informed the Albion crew that the Northern crew was unable to go on with the race because one of his men had left. He did not forfeit the binding money because the contest was meant to be a friendly. Although it is not mentioned in the report of this meeting, within two weeks it becomes obvious that the man who has abandoned ship is Renforth, and he will waste no time before joining the Albion Rowing club.

The Durham Regatta at the end of June was Renforth's next target. He was entered for the Brancepeth Plate, a skiff race, open to all; entrance 2s. 6d; one mile and a quarter; for a purse of £5, and £2 to the second boat. It was always good to win money, but the purse was relatively small – the important thing about the Brancepeth Plate this year was that Renforth would come up against James Taylor.

Taylor and Renforth were drawn together in the first heat and before the start Renforth was anything but happy with the condition of his skiff, and complained bitterly that his left-hand oar was sprung (split) a little. Taylor's boat was some 7 lbs lighter than Renforth's, a significant difference since that would represent about 20 per cent of the weight of the boat. It was possible to transport boats by rail, or by steamer, but it cost. At this time the North Eastern Railway Company was offering to transport rowers and their boats on a double journey for a single fare, but it still cost 2d a mile to send a boat by rail. In 1869 it cost Tynemouth Amateur Rowing Club 10s 4d to transport their boats by rail to Durham Station, without any consideration of the cost of taking boats between the station and the river. It was cheaper to borrow a boat from one of the home clubs at the regatta, but Renforth's difficulties before his heat with Taylor indicate the potential drawbacks of that course of action.

Betting was first at 6 to 4 on Renforth, but switched to even money when Taylor won the toss and took the inside station. Choice of station was important because the River Wear at Durham provides a twisting awkward course and fouling was a regular feature of the regatta. Taylor took the lead at the start, but after the pair had left Pelaw

Wood Renforth put on a magnificent spurt and went from half a length down to a quarter of a length up within 50 yards. He dominated the rest of the race, relaxing as he increased his lead and shouting out to Taylor to 'come on', eventually winning easily by 100 yards. Afterwards the pair shook hands and Taylor acknowledged that he had been beaten by 'a thundering good man'. Renforth won the final easily, beating John Appleby, with Robert Chambers (Wallsend) again demonstrating the difficulties of competing on a 'foreign' river, when he was unable to find a boat in which to row by the time of the start!

The following day, 1st July , Renforth rowed the four oar race in a scratch Albion 2nd crew, stroked by James Percy. They put up a poor performance but the significance of this event is the appearance of Renforth in an Albion crew for the first time.

The Durham Regatta of 1868 was a milestone in the development of James Renforth as a rower and as a sculler. He had beaten the highly rated James Taylor easily, despite rowing in an inferior skiff. He had appeared for the first time at a regatta rowing in a four-oar, and what is more he had represented the Albion Club, which was the club of the Champion crew. James Taylor, who was a member of the Champion crew, now knew exactly how good Renforth was, and, with his usual financial acumen, had only lost a 2s 6d entrance fee in finding that out! Renforth could now look forward to the second half of 1868 with every confidence.

# Championship Contender

Renforth now embarked on a round of regatta appearances. He was still not matched and looked set to tour the country, racing for small purses, unless a suitable opponent could be persuaded to take him on. The week after the Durham Regatta he could be found in Sunderland, competing for a first prize of £6 over a $1^{1/4}$ mile course. In his first heat he was again due to race against James Taylor, who pragmatically withdrew. John Appleby of the Wear, and his old rival James Boyd of Gateshead, contested the final with him but he won as he chose by five lengths. The week after that, from Saturday 11th to Tuesday 14th July 1868, he was in Leeds, losing the final of a handicap race on the Monday when he ran into the bank. It was not Renforth's day because later in the afternoon he was disqualified from a canoe race! He must eventually have mastered the course because on the Tuesday he won the open skiff race, the Aire Stakes, and collected a very welcome £25 for his efforts.

While the regatta season was progressing, the Renforths welcomed a new addition to the family. Mary gave birth to a baby girl, Margaret Jane, on 23rd June 1868 at 6, Church Street, Gateshead. Margaret Jane was also the name James and Mary had given their first-born child, who had died back in January 1863, aged only 7 months. On this occasion the second Margaret Jane survived for only 3 weeks before succumbing to 'tabes', emaciation, on the 14th July. One assumes she just failed to thrive, and, according to the register entry, James was present when she died. This meant he must have returned from his victory that day in Leeds just in time to witness the death of his baby daughter. It is impossible to piece together what this time was like for the Renforths, but pleasure at James's increasing success on the water must have been tempered by sadness at the loss of another child.

On Saturday 25th July 1868 James left Newcastle by steamer for London accompanied by the champion four-oared crew, James Taylor, Matthew Scott, Andrew Thompson and Robert Chambers (stroke), to take part in the Thames National Regatta, starting on the 4th August. Once the Tyneside lads were in the capital the Putney towpath was abuzz with speculation that Renforth was a true flyer who would put the London scullers, even the champion Kelley, on their mettle. Indeed Kelley was threatening to withdraw, objecting to the skiff race being billed as the Championship of the Thames. As the accepted Champion of the Thames he felt that anybody who wished to wrest the title from him should row a match against him alone. He did agree to compete however, but having been beaten in the first heat by James Percy, he declined a privileged opportunity to compete in the final against Renforth, Percy and Joseph Sadler.

The Regatta was a triumph for the Northcountrymen, with Renforth winning the sculls, and £90, Taylor and Scott taking the pair-oar championship, and Chambers, Thompson, Scott and Taylor coming home as victors in the four-oared race. Today it would have been as if Newcastle United had won the Premier League and the FA Cup, within a few days of each other! At the risk of baffling those readers who have never lived on Tyneside, I reproduce in full a music hall song of the time, 'Defeat O' the Cocknies', a title which gets right to the point, I think you will agree, written to commemorate the victories of the Tynesiders. Since there were no tabloid newspapers it was quite usual to disseminate versions of current events to the general public in the form of popular songs delivered at music halls. Renforth seems to have attended music halls regularly and indeed on the night of the 7th August he was spotted in the audience at the Oxford Music Hall by General Tom Dot and invited up on stage to shake hands. When he came forward the audience greeted him with hearty cheers and the chairman, Mr Thompson, thanked the audience on his behalf. The Oxford Music Hall building still stands in the centre of Newcastle, just to the east of the Laing Art Gallery, and is currently a nightclub.

## THE DEFEAT O' THE COCKNIES
## BE THE COALLY TYNE HEROES, AT THAMES GRAND REGATTA, AUGUST 4TH AND 5TH, 1868

*(TEUN – 'Barbary Bell,' or the 'Wunderful Tallegraff.')*

AW'LL sing ye a bit sang if ye'll join i' the korus,
Ye'll give us a gud un, – aw's sartin ye will,
For it's all i' the praise i' the Coally Tyne heroes,
The Champeins we've had, an' the Champeins we've still;
Tho aw's sad when aw think o' brave honest Bob Chambers,
Aw's glad the example he set's been weel tyen,
For wor bonny boat-pullers, the best of a' scullers,
Thor lickt for thor equal, – becas they heh nyen.

Noo it's mony a lang eer since game aud Harry Clasper
Astonish'd the Cocknies, an' myed them fight shy,
The Tyneside boat-rowers, se prood o' thor river,

Kept up the successes for eers its gyen by;
Then Chambers, the Champein ov' a' the world's pullers,
Goh the Cocknies a gliff that they'll nivor forget,
Whey, Kelley for six eers dor hardly gan near him,
Till he knew Bob was deun, – then he challinsed wor pet!

But lads, thor's still gud uns withoot gan te Lundin,
An' where will ye find them but just on the Tyne?
Did ye ivor hear owt like the greet Thames Regatta?
Where the canny Tynesiders se bonny did shine;
Aw wad like te been there te seen a' the lang fyeces,
The Cocknies wad pull when they fund they war deun,
For they nivor imadjind the whole o' the prizes,
For Champeins, wad cum te wor river as seun.

Thor wes game Jimmy Taylor, Mat Scott, Andrew Thompson,
Wi' the second Bob Chambers te pull the stroke oar,
Com in for the Hundrid withoot ony trubbil, –
Twes easier then ivor its been wun afore;
Then the race for the Pairs, tho twes reckund a grand un,
Just show'd o' what hard stuff a Tynesider's myed,
For Taylor an' Scott fairly bothered a' Lundin,-
'Gox! Wor gan te get nowt this time!' Kelley then said.

But the Champeinship race is wor pride an' wor glory,
When brave Jimmy Renforth, se honest an' true,
Led the way before gud men like Sadler an' Percy,
An' the foaks that wes there really sweer that he flew!
He's Champein ov Ingland, – then wish him success, lads,
May he, like poor Bob Chambers, stick weel te the nyem;
Then gud luck te the Fowers, the Pairs, an' the Champein,
Besides a' the canny boat-pullers at hyem!

Renforth's confidence, and no doubt that of his backers, was boosted by his success on the Thames, and a challenge to Kelley appeared in the *Newcastle Daily Chronicle* of Saturday August 8th, 1868 (see following page).

As one would expect there now followed some skirmishing by letter. Kelley was not happy about Renforth claiming the title, 'champion of the Thames' and did not wish to surrender the advantage of rowing on his home river. He was adamant that the

## CHALLENGE OF RANDFORD TO KELLEY.

JAMES RANDFORD (champion of the Thames) is open to row Henry Kelley, of Putney, London (two months from the first deposit), on the Tyne, or any neutral water, for the Championship of England and £200 a-side. The Editor of the *Newcastle Daily Chronicle* to be stakeholder. Articles and a deposit to the *Chronicle* office will be attended to.

*The challenge of 8th August 1868.*

match would not go ahead unless Renforth agreed to row on the Thames championship course, from Putney to Mortlake. Renforth suggested rowing on a neutral course at King's Lynn, or offered Kelley £20 expenses to come to the Tyne. Kelley held firm and also refused to row 'home and home' matches, one on the Thames and one on the Tyne. Meanwhile Renforth continued to gain experience by racing at the Chester Regatta, where for the first time he appeared as a member of the Champion four. Robert Chambers was the man left out, with James Taylor switching to stroke and Renforth rowing bow. The new four was, James Renforth, Matthew Scott, Andrew Thompson and James Taylor (stroke). The fours race, and £40, was won in what was said to be the quickest time on record, and Renforth also won the sculls, and £10, beating James Taylor by the suspiciously close margin of a quarter of a length. For the moment no agreement could be reached as to where and when Renforth and Kelley would cross blades, but Kelley gave up the running of his public house in Putney to concentrate on rowing.

At the end of August the Champion crew, with Renforth still rowing bow, won the watermen's prize of £30 at the Burton-on-Trent Regatta. Later, in a novelty race, Renforth again proved an incompetent canoeist, being beaten into third place by his team mates Thompson and Taylor. Mat Scott fell out of his canoe half way and was disqualified, but undaunted he entertained the crowd with some fancy swimming!

On Tuesday, September 8th 1868 Renforth and his backers met at James Taylor's, the Trafalgar Inn, New Bridge Street, Newcastle, to make a few minor changes to the proposed articles sent through by Kelley. The Northerners had conceded the choice of course to the champion and the match would take place on the Thames. The location of the backers' meeting was significant in that it showed how much of an influence James Taylor had become on Renforth. It is difficult to say precisely when Renforth switched his allegiance from Messrs Brown and Stewart to James Taylor. These matters were inevitably conducted in secret, but the defection of Renforth from the Northern

Rowing Club four-oar around the 22nd June probably marked the start of a perceptible link between Taylor and James Renforth. It also explained why Taylor so happily acknowledged that he had been beaten by the better man, immediately after his humiliating defeat at the hands of Renforth in the skiff race at the Durham Regatta. At the meeting on the 8th September, Renforth was able to sign the articles himself – he had begun to learn how to read and write, perhaps with the encouragement of his friend, fellow oarsman and now backer, James Taylor, although he still did not know how to spell his own name!

The final articles of agreement were as follows:

**Articles of agreement between Henry Kelley, of Putney, on the one part, and James Renforth, of Gateshead, on the other part. They hereby agree to row a right-away scullers race from Putney to the Ship, at Mortlake, for £200 a-side and the Championship of England. To start from two boats moored twenty yards apart opposite the 'Star and Garter'. The steamboats to be behind the men at starting. The race to take place on Tuesday, the 17th November, according to the recognised laws of boat racing. The referee to be chosen at the last deposit. In the event of the men not agreeing, two to be named, who must be drawn for, and whose decision shall be final. Cutters accompanying the men to keep astern of the sternmost man. The first deposit of £25 a-side is now (11th September) in the hands of 'Bell's Life,' who shall be final stakeholder; the next deposit of £25 a-side on Friday, the 2nd of October at 'Bell's Life;' the third deposit of £50 a-side, 23rd October at 'Bell's Life:' the fourth deposit of £50 a-side, on the 6th November; and the last deposit of £50 a-side to be made at the Bells Tavern, Putney, on Thursday, the 12th November, between seven and nine p.m. The referee to be starter. Either party failing to comply with these conditions to forfeit the money down. – (Signed) Jas. Randford, H. Kelley. Witnesses – James Taylor, Charles Bush.**

Both Kelley and Renforth immediately started training for the event. Kelley went to the seaside at Margate to take advantage of the healthy sea air, but it did not help him much as he caught a cold and soon returned to Putney, where thereafter his training progressed satisfactorily.

Renforth moved from his home in Gateshead to James Taylor's house, the Trafalgar Inn, since Taylor was not only a backer, but had also agreed to train Renforth for the championship contest. This is the first time that Renforth seems to have had any sort of formal training arrangement. He was largely a self-taught oarsman and sculler, but no doubt picked up knowledge on the river from whatever source he could.

In the early days he was managed by the Boyd brothers and often trained alongside the elder brother James. Taylor soon discovered that training Renforth would be no easy task. After only a few days of good food and moderate work on the river Renforth had begun to put on flesh alarmingly. Extreme measures would be needed to remove the weight and harden his muscular frame sufficiently to produce him in a fit condition for the championship race.

Taylor and Renforth therefore moved to Mr Brown's, the Dun Cow Inn, Dunston, for about a fortnight, from where they took their daily outings on the river, and their land exercise. Taylor was matched with Mark Addy for £50 a-side, to race on the Tyne on 19th October , so he needed to train himself as well as tend to the needs of his charge. The Dun Cow remains a public house and the locals are still interested in sport, although these days conversation is concentrated on football and in particular the fortunes of Newcastle United. Paul Gascoigne, 'Gazza', the former Newcastle, Tottenham, Rangers, Middlesbrough, Everton and England star, hails from Dunston and patronises the historic old pub on his visits to Tyneside. The traditional Dun Cow on the pub sign wears a black and white shirt!

Taylor did not need such hard training as Renforth so he enlisted the help of Mr John Adams and other friends to give the required extra training on land. After Taylor had completed his race against Addy, which he won on a foul, the pair returned to the Trafalgar and Renforth finished off his Tyneside preparation from there. By 2nd November supporters could purchase his colours from the Trafalgar and make a public show of whom they favoured in the forthcoming tussle. Rowing colours took the form of a silk handkerchief, usually embroidered with some sort of commemorative design. Renforth's handkerchief for the match against Kelley was white, with a double blue border, an anchor in each corner, and '1868' also in blue, in the centre. The issuing of colours worked in a similar way to the marketing of football strips today, and provided a useful secondary income for oarsmen. Colours were designed and offered for sale whenever there was a major race. The usual charge for the handkerchief was 1 guinea (£1 1s.), and that remained the fee if the man, or crew, you favoured won the race. If you were purchasing the colours after the race, and your favourite had lost, you were allowed to give what you pleased, but it was considered ungentlemanly to offer less than the cost of the material. Frequently a guinea was given, win or lose.

Seven of this type of 'colours' handkerchief from the 1870s and 1880s have survived to become part of the collections of Tyne and Wear Museums. They are very large and we would certainly describe them today as silk scarves. I am not aware of any surviving 'colours' handkerchieves that were issued for James Renforth's races, although a photograph of James taken in Canada in 1871 shows him stripped to the

*Henry Kelley*

waist with one tied round his neck.

For Renforth's main financial backers it was time to get a good indication of their man's chances, without alerting the 'touts'. Early in the morning, ten days before the race, Renforth rowed a two mile trial on the Tyne and recorded an excellent time. He was ready to take on the Champion. Occasionally rumours had circulated that Renforth was unwell, but this was all part of the build-up to any big race. Even a cold could be alarming, since with no antibiotics any secondary infection was likely to destroy a sculler's chance.

A week before the race, Taylor left for London on the early (2am) train to prepare Renforth's quarters at the Duke's Head, Putney. Renforth, accompanied by John Adams, took the afternoon train at 1.50pm and was cheered on his way by hundreds of well-wishers who had gathered at Newcastle Central Station. The next morning, Wednesday 11th November, Taylor and Renforth were out on the river, rowing the whole course from Putney to Mortlake. It was misty and at intervals Renforth was

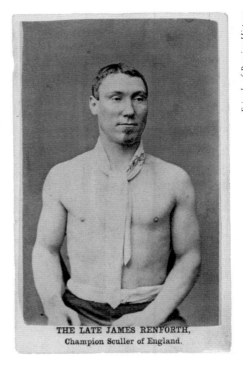

THE LATE JAMES RENFORTH,
Champion Sculler of England.

*James Renforth stripped to the waist in a portrait taken just before his final race in 1871. He is in hard condition and has the English four's colours handkerchief around his neck.*

able to row flat out without alerting the touts on the river bank, who, with their view obscured by the mist, could see very little. For the rest of his time in London he was guarded in his training on the river, taking it easy or rowing a very fast stroke without really putting on the power. Many observers were unimpressed and likened him to Hamill, the American rower whose fast stroke had flattered to deceive. When Hamill had challenged for the championship on the Tyne in 1866 he had been beaten soundly by Kelley. This was all good news for those planning to bet on Renforth – in most of his contests on the Tyne he had been the odds-on favourite. Even with Renforth hiding his true abilities the gambling on the race was at even money, with just the occasional wager at 5 to 4 on Kelley, but only for small sums.

The rest of the Tyne party arrived on Monday, led by William Blakey, landlord of

*Colours handkerchief from a race in 1880 of R.W. Boyd, the son of James Boyd.*

the Adelaide Hotel and J.H. Baird of the Star Hotel. James Percy, who had been fancied as the next champion from the Tyne before Renforth burst on the scene, was there, and John Hawks Clasper, old Harry's son, who was now building boats in Wandsworth, was also in attendance. John Hawks Clasper joined James Taylor on the river in a double scull to assist in some last minute work on Renforth's starting technique.

Race day was Tuesday 17th November and there was competition for the attention of Londoners in the form of a Parliamentary election. The crowd which attended the race was smaller than those that had watched the previous three championship contests. The *Newcastle Daily Chronicle*'s account of the race, published on Wednesday 18th November 1868, gives a full description of the scene, with the riverside working class in the largest attendance, out on the Thames in all manner of craft. Many of the men would have been enfranchised by the Reform Act of the previous year but perhaps they were so unfamiliar with the concept of voting that they had not bothered to exercise their democratic choice, or maybe they had voted earlier in the day. In any case none of the women were eligible to vote.

**Upon the water the plebian element of society was, in fact, by far the most largely represented, the riverside porters, herring curers, and fish and fruit sellers, turning out in strong force. Many of the rickety craft, propelled along by the strong arms of half-a-dozen 'costers', bore with it a blooming burden of wives, sweethearts, and children, and sounds of voluble talking, occasionally varied by volleys of hearty laughter, fell upon the river breeze as the boats passed cheerily along.**

The race was due off soon after 3pm and shortly before the start the principal supporters made their way by means of sculler boats to the official steamer, and further betting took place. At the last moment the odds veered round to 5 to 4 on Renforth and Mr Charles Bush, Kelley's major backer, took £21 to £20 six times over. That is he risked losing £120 if Kelley lost but would win £126 from the supporters of Renforth if Kelley won.

Renforth was weighed at the Duke's Head, fully clothed but for his hat and coat, and tipped the scales at 11st 5lbs. Stripped to his rowing costume he would have been about 10st 12lbs. Kelley was prepared at his own house, a short distance across the fields from the river at Putney. He weighed 10st 6lbs when stripped for the race.

At five minutes to three Renforth stepped into his new skiff, the *Alderman Cowen M.P.*, which had been built for him a month previously by Robert Jewitt of Dunston. The outside shell was of cedar wood and the dimensions were as follows:

| | |
|---|---|
| Length | 30 feet |
| Width amidships | $11^{3}/_{4}$ inches |
| Height at stem | $3^{3}/_{4}$ inches |
| Height at stern | $2^{7}/_{8}$ inches |
| Height amidships | $5^{1}/_{2}$ inches |
| Weight | 30 lbs |

He was wearing a tight fitting jersey and a scarlet cap and quickly rowed out close to the bow of the referee's boat. As he approached the steamer he was greeted with loud cheers from the Newcastle party aboard and, lifting his cap, he bowed in recognition of this reception. The referee, Mr Ireland, leaned over the bow and told Renforth that if there was a foul he was to continue rowing and allow him, the referee, to decide the outcome. Renforth held up his hand and quickly replied, 'I will give way, sir, sooner

*Bird's-eye view of the Thames Championship course in 1875, from the Illustrated London News.*

than there shall be any foul. I will do as you tell me'. His straightforward manner and expression of honest intentions were applauded by those who witnessed the conversation. Kelley took to the water soon after Renforth, also in a new Jewitt-built craft, *Violet*, the name reflecting Harry Kelley's choice of rowing colours.

Renforth won the toss for choice of station and, selecting the Middlesex or north side, rather facetiously, but perhaps as a result of nerves, cried out 'I have won the match then'.

Both men were cheered as they rowed away to their respective eight-oared cutters to strip. Renforth's cutter was manned by Thames watermen with J.H. Clasper steering and James Taylor lying in the bow to pilot his young protégé over the course. Renforth also had a four-oar in attendance, rowed by London professionals, whose job it was to row slightly in advance and outside of him to prevent the encroachment of any unruly steamboats. Renforth was the first to strip, characteristically doing vigorous stretching exercises before rowing away with the short quick strokes for which the Londoners had so little time. Kelley soon followed and, at a signal from the referee, both men rowed to the middle of the stream and backed onto their respective stakeboats. After one false start from Kelley they got away for a perfect start at about 3.20pm.

Renforth started fast, with a very high rating, but soon settling to his work he drove his boat forward with an exceptionally powerful, finely finished action of the oar and nosed in front after only half a dozen strokes. Two hundred yards from the start he had a lead of nearly a third of a length. The short, quick, uneven strokes he had rowed in the previous week to confuse the river touts had gone and been replaced by his uniquely powerful style of rowing. To quote the *Chronicle*:

> ... bending right forward he took a magnificent hold of the water, and drawing the stroke fairly home with all the combined power of his muscular arms and loins, he made his skiff absolutely fly through the water with a steady ceaseless motion. There was now not a single trace of the fear and almost boyish lightness which had distinguished him before the start; but with close-set and resolute countenance he rose and fell to his stroke with the smoothness, rapidity, and regularity of a steam engine.

Kelley rowed in a much more orthodox style, with straight arms and back, and none of the sliding, thigh-thrusting activity of Renforth. His friends were convinced that Renforth could not keep up his all-action stroke for the full length of the course and urged their man to keep going and be ready for the inevitable collapse of the northerner.

After only a quarter of a mile the referee's boat was unable to keep up and the Thames steamboat skippers, who had an unenviable reputation for unruliness, and even foul play, churned their craft forward to within a few feet of the accompanying cutters. The referee was therefore unable to see the race at all from now on! Fortunately he was not required to adjudicate on any foul play and the race continued without him. The principal supporters, having laid out a tidy sum to be aboard the official boat, now had to view the rest of the race through binoculars!

Renforth was now rowing 40 strokes to the minute and as he approached Bishop's Creek, about one third of a mile into the race, he had a lead of a length. The Newcastle men roared him on, while on the banks and aboard the steamers the London crowd was silent. At Craven Point Renforth was two lengths ahead but as the Surrey bend opened up Kelley spurted and cut back Renforth's lead by half a length. For a moment there was the risk of a foul but Renforth did not give way. Seeing the difficulty, he responded aggressively with a surge of his own, and, going two lengths up again, he took Kelley's Surrey station and gave the champion the added problem of rowing in his wash. Kelley dug in, but at the Hammersmith Suspension Bridge ($1^3/_4$ miles) Renforth was still two lengths ahead and had completed the distance in eight minutes 50 seconds, about the fastest time on record, and nearly a minute quicker than Chambers and Sadler had done it in their contest on the Thames.

Passing the Hammersmith Lead Mills, Kelley made another bid for victory but Renforth once again responded with a spurt of his own and the champion was unable to make any impression. At Chiswick Eyot Renforth's lead was three lengths and the race was virtually over bar an accident to the Tynesider. He had it in his power to leave Kelley when he chose but Renforth preferred to row within himself on what, after all, was still an unfamiliar river to him, and just keep his opponent at a safe distance. At Barnes Bridge Renforth was still three lengths up and after that he sculled as he pleased, passing the winning post four lengths to the good. The winning time was 22 minutes and 35 seconds and as he rowed back to his cutter to collect his clothes Renforth was neither sweating nor out of breath. In contrast poor Kelley finished physically distressed and depressed by his defeat. Both men dressed and were then received aboard the referee's boat.

Back in Newcastle a crowd had begun to congregate in front of the offices of the *Chronicle* at about the time that the match was due off. By five o'clock there were 7,000 people gathered there and passage through the streets round about was impossible. At ten past five the news of Renforth's victory was received and was conveyed to the crowd by the posting of a short note in the window. A volley of cheering came from the gathering and men ran around in a frenzy of delight amid scenes of uncontrolled enthusiasm. A large crowd had also gathered in front of James Taylor's house, the Trafalgar Inn, and as soon as news of the victory reached there a string of flags was hung across the street. In the evening all the sporting pubs were crowded and the only topic of conversation was Renforth's fantastic championship triumph.

In London that evening Renforth was presented with a victor's wreath at the Canterbury Music Hall, appearing on stage with Kelley, Taylor, Drewitt (the well-known London professional oarsman) and J.H. Clasper. The Londoners had no complaints and accepted that the best man had won. The crowd gave three cheers for Renforth and Kelley and the two men made short speeches. Renforth said that he was proud to have won the championship of the world and he believed that no other man in England was capable of beating Kelley. Kelley said that he had been beaten by a good man but hoped he would be successful in his next match (he was engaged to row against Joseph Sadler).

It is perhaps worth a mention as to why two men, one from the Tyne and one from the Thames should reckon that the winner of their contest could claim to be the

Champion of the World. The answer lay in the recent history of the championship. Over the first 30 years of boat racing in England the national championship had been contested between firstly the men of the Thames, and soon after that, the men of the Thames and the Tyne. However in 1863 Bob Chambers had taken on, and beaten, Green of Australia and the title of 'World Champion' first gained currency. Kelley's defeat of the American Hamill in 1866 had added further weight to the claim of global superiority. Renforth, as the conqueror of Kelley, (who of course had taken the title by defeating Chambers in 1865) seemed therefore to have every right to call himself champion of the world.

Renforth returned to Tyneside a hero and was welcomed by 10,000 people when he arrived at Newcastle Central Station just before 5pm on Thursday 19th November. Some of the crowd had clambered up on to the ledges at the bases of the columns in the portico of the station in order to get a better view. Despite his protestations and muscular efforts to resist, the new champion was pinched, touched, and eventually borne shoulder high to his cab. His travelling cap was removed and a laurel wreath was put on his head. As soon as he got to the cab he took the wreath off! He obviously felt quite uncomfortable about all this adulation. The crowd refused to let the cab leave so the horse was unharnessed and the crowd drew the cab through the streets to the Trafalgar Inn, New Bridge Street, a distance of about half a mile. The Trafalgar was then mobbed until Renforth appeared at one of the hotel windows and said a few words. The bars were packed all evening with people hoping to catch a glimpse of James Renforth.

Renforth's backers were delighted with the manner in which the touts had been fooled and the *Chronicle* even gloated a little at how the London press had also been taken in. Renforth was feted wherever he went and now Newcastle people were saying of Renforth what they had once said about Bob Chambers, 'He's not a human being, he's an engine. He was cast at Hawks's and fitted at Stephenson's.'

The inevitable celebratory music hall song was swiftly composed and was no doubt warmly received all over Tyneside.

## RENFORTH, THE CHAMPEIN

*(TEUN – 'The Postman's Knock.')*

Tyneside's lang been fam'd for producin greet men,
Luck at Airmstrang an' Stivvison, tee,
An' Grainger that myed wor fine toon what it is,
An' its bildins thor grand ye'll agree;
But the bildin o' boats an' boat pullin's wor pride,

An' where, always we try hard te shine, –
An' Renforth, a brave hardy Son o' the North's
Browt the Champeinship back te the Tyne.

*Korus*
*Then lang may success an' gud hilth combine*
*Wi' Renforth, the Champein o' Thames an' the Tyne.*

We lost poor Bob Chambers, then sadly we greev'd,
Thor wes nyen but what liked Honest Bob,
An' we sigh'd for anuther te fill up he's place,
Tho' we knew twes a difficult job,
Till Renforth com oot like the man that he is,
For the honour o' canny Tyneside,
An' te stop him frae tyekin Bob Chambers's place,
The whole world he bravely defied!

Then a challinse wes sent, an' a match thor wes myed
Wi' the best Lundun Champein thor's been,
That's brave Harry Kelley, the Pride o' the Thames,
An' a finer race nivor wes seen;
For wi' confidence pictor'd on each manly broo'
The North an' the South meet agyen,
Thor ready! – thor off! – then the struggle begins
As the crowd roar an' cheer for thor men.

Incorridg'd be cheers frae thor frinds all aroond,
Thor byeth strivin hard for the leed,
An' then the North Countrymen shoot wi' delight,
As they see thor pet forgin aheed,
Tho Kelley, as game as man ivor can be,
Spurts hard te catch Jimmy, but nay!
The Tynesider's there wi' byeth corridge an' skill,
Ay, an' strength tee te leed a' the way.

The Champeinship's wun, an it's browt te the Tyne,
A river myed famous wi' men
Like Chambers, the Claspers, Bob Cooper, besides
Jimmy Taylor, an' Percy, – so then
Gud luck te Jim Renforth, lang may he maintain

The honour he noo hauds wi' pride;
An' gud luck tiv his trainer, Jim Taylor, as weel,
An' the boat-pullers a' roond Tyneside!

Renforth enjoyed the limelight that his championship brought, but he was less than confident in his abilities as a public speaker. He had a strong Geordie accent and when invited to speak always tried to keep his utterances short. Celebration dinners and appearances on stage at theatres and music halls were all very well, but Renforth was a professional boat rower and he needed regular matches to keep up his income. His dismantling of Harry Kelley over a championship course meant he was unlikely to find any takers for a straightforward sculling race. At a gathering in the Bridge End Hotel, Newcastle his old adversary James Boyd, who had held the lead for the first few hundred yards of their race in 1867, offered to row a £10 a-side match from the High Level Bridge to the Skinner Burn, a distance of about 600 yards. Waterside opinion said that Renforth was a slow starter, so a man who was fast away might be able to hold him off over a short distance. At the same meeting a contest was proposed between Robert Boyd and James Renforth's younger brother Stephen from the High Level Bridge to the Scotswood Suspension Bridge for a stake of £50. James posted the binding money for Stephen.

James Renforth would need to look beyond the boat rowers of the Tyne if he was to secure another lucrative high stakes race. In a letter to the *Chronicle* (see facing page) on 1st December 1868 he set out the circumstances under which he was prepared to defend his title and also maintained the stance he had adopted in his exchanges with Kelley as to how the championship of the Thames should be decided.

For the moment the proposed race with James Boyd fell through and Renforth continued with his round of dinners, receptions and presentations of gifts of a signet ring, a medal or a silver goblet to mark the occasion of his victory over Kelley. Sometimes a purse of gold would be added to the commemorative gift, which provided immediate income, but what the champion was to do henceforth was of some concern, obviously to him, but to others as well.

The *Chronicle* columnist 'Elswick', recognising Renforth's potential financial embarrassment, wrote a piece suggesting an annual contest for the championship of the Tyne among boat rowers resident on Tyneside. The prize for the winner would be sufficient to provide a reasonable annual income. The expectation would be that Renforth would win it for many years to come, and so would not be forced to return to his former work as a blacksmith's striker. The other advantage as far as 'Elswick' was concerned was that there would be no need for supporters of rowing to try and set

Renforth up as a publican: a route which had been tried with earlier Tyneside aquatic heroes, with little success. The qualities which were needed to make a successful oarsman were quite different from those required to prosper in the licensed trade.

In early December Renforth put out a speculative 'Challenge to the World' through the *Chronicle* offering a £200 a-side contest on the Tyne Championship course. Since he received no immediate response he probably tried to garner a little local action by making some sort of handicap challenge in the 1868 Boxing Day edition of the *Chronicle*, to which John Bright responded with a proposal for an open boat contest. Bright wanted to race for £25 a-side over a mile course but wanted a handicap of 50 yards, roughly five lengths, at the start. This would enable him to take Renforth's water immediately, give the champion the benefit of his back wash, block any move to overtake and even have some chance of claiming a foul if Renforth collided with him in trying to get past. No oarsman or his backers fancied taking Renforth on over a championship distance, or over any distance, on level terms. Even as Renforth won the championship and acknowledged the acclaim of the crowd his authoritative performance had marked him down as an opponent to be avoided.

---

## AQUATICS.
### THE AQUATIC CHAMPIONSHIP.
#### *To the Editor of the Daily Chronicle.*

SIR,—I, James Renforth, having won the title of Champion Sculler of England, by defeating Henry Kelley, of Putney, on the Thames, on 17th instant, do hereby give notice that I am prepared to defend my right thereto against all persons disputing my ability to hold the same ; and that I shall only contest that title on the river Tyne, as I am firmly of opinion that an aquatic champion, in addition to the title, is justly entitled, until defeated, to have the Championship races rowed on the river of which he is the representative. And I hereby further give notice that I place at the disposal of the Thames National Regatta Committee the title of Champion of the Thames, now held by me, to be rowed for at their Annual Regatta ; reserving to myself the right of entering for such race.—Dated this 1st day of December, 1868.—(Signed)
      JAMES RENFORTH, Champion of England.
   Newcastle-on-Tyne.

# Fame and Mixed Fortune – 1869

The New Year was only a few days old when James Renforth found that being the champion sculler of the world did not ensure a smooth passage through the social and legal niceties of life. Renforth's younger brother Stephen was matched to row a sculling race against Robert Boyd for £25 a-side on the 23rd January, and by New Year's Day £20 of the stake had been deposited. On that day Stephen had been struck by a waterman named Thomas Maddison, supposedly for his impudence, and, according to Renforth, Maddison had gone on to say, 'Go and fetch your champion brother.' The champion brother had caught up with Maddison in Errington's public house, Newgate Street, Newcastle on the night of Sunday 3rd January. The evidence of what exactly took place is conflicting but there is no dispute that Renforth struck the first blow: even a witness called by the champion reluctantly had to admit that this was so. The result of the two men coming together was a cut eye for Maddison, which on the 6th January was still closed from the force of the blow. The damage was all the greater because Renforth was wearing two rings on one of the fingers of the hand with which he struck Maddison. The prosecuting solicitor, Mr Joel, said that, 'He understood that the defendant was the champion rower, and did not know whether he was the champion pugilist or not; but at any rate, on this occasion he had acted more like a pugilist than a rower.'

It would be easy to dismiss this as a drunken brawl started by a champion who had an exaggerated view of his own importance and a primitive approach to family loyalty. That would be a mistake. Witnesses to the fight testified that neither man was drunk. Renforth's real concern seems to have been that, with £20 down and the match only three weeks away, if Stephen had been badly hurt the £20 stake money would have been forfeit. In professional rowing circles it was bad business to strike a man who was matched and had a large sum of money at stake.

The magistrates at the Newcastle Police Court, which is where Renforth found himself on the 6th January, were not impressed with the champion's version of events. They were certain that Renforth had gone to Errington's for the purpose of picking a quarrel and that if his brother had had a grievance against Maddison he should have brought it to them. They could not allow even the champion sculler to take the law into his own hands, so they fined him 40 shillings with costs.

*James Taylor. A fine sculler, who was just too light to reach the very top. Taylor coached Renforth to the sculling championship in 1868. After the split with Renforth in 1870 he formed a crew with Tom Winship, Bob Bagnall and Joseph Sadler.*

The fine was paid immediately.

The report of the court proceedings ends, 'The defendant complained that he could not get walked in the streets without being annoyed by these parties.' Which seems a bit rich when one considers that Renforth had sought out the unlucky and now somewhat bloodied and bruised Maddison!

It was a disputatious start to the year for James Renforth. While he was still smarting from his New Year brush with the law, he became embroiled in an argument over the make up of the Champion Four. At a reception held in a Gateshead public house to honour Renforth for winning the championship, James Taylor was heard to make some remarks that were interpreted as meaning that he was thinking of altering the line-up of the Champion Four. He later denied that this was his intention but a split opened up between James Taylor (stroke) and James Renforth (bow) on the one hand, and the midships powerhouses Matt Scott and Andrew Thompson on the other. Scott and Thompson were the first to go into print about the dispute in the *Chronicle* of January 5th but Taylor was quick to respond in the next day's paper declaring that he had never intended for one moment to break up the Champion Four, but since Scott and Thompson had been so hasty as to issue a challenge … Taylor offered a four-oared race for £50 a-side: Scott and Thompson plus two other men of their choice versus Taylor and Renforth and two men of their choice. All the rowers had to be from the Tyne. As an alternative Taylor offered a pair-oared race for £25 a-side, with Taylor and Renforth engaged in a straight contest with Thompson and Scott.

A cynic might argue that this internecine dispute at about the turn of the year was a handy device for injecting interest in the Tyneside rowing scene at a time when things were normally slack as regards top class racing. A study of Taylor's long career reveals him to have been astute at manipulating the business side of professional rowing and it would have been in character for him to have engineered the schism. He may well have suckered Scott and Thompson into making the challenge so he could even claim that it had not been him who split the four. Since all the antagonists are long dead we shall never know, but, whatever the real cause of the dispute, after about a week of wrangling it was agreed to row a pair-oar race for £50 a-side on Monday 25th January 1869.

Both pairs went into hard training immediately since race day was only two weeks away. The astute Taylor now put Renforth into the stroke seat, recognising how much James had progressed since last summer. Public interest in the contest was intense. Could the plucky little publican and his champion protégé defeat the heavyweights who had formed the engine room of the all conquering Champion Four? Compared with the giants who row today they were all small men, but Scott and Thompson were significantly bigger and heavier than their opponents.

| | Height | Weight | Age |
|---|---|---|---|
| James Taylor | 5ft 7½in | 10st 5lb | 32 years |
| James Renforth | 5ft 7½in | 11st 5lb | 26 years |
| Matthew Scott | 5ft 9½in | 11st 10lb | 33 years |
| Andrew Thompson | 5ft 10½in | 12st 6lb | 28 years |

Renforth and Taylor had the use of the old champion pair boat, the *Robert Chambers*, a very fine craft built by Robert Jewitt of Dunston about 12 months previously. Scott and Thompson had no suitable boat in which to practise or race and were fortunate to be lent the club pair, *Ariel,* by the Northern Rowing Club committee, although it was a little bit short in length for the two heavyweights. Nonetheless they soon had *Ariel* going well in training and declared themselves confident of victory in the upcoming contest.

As well as preparing for his own pair oar race, James Renforth had to oversee the training of his younger brother Stephen for the match with Robert Boyd, which was to take place two days before the showdown between the members of the Champion Four. Antagonism had continued between the Boyds and the Renforths and this contest had stemmed from a chance meeting of Stephen and Robert Boyd in the bar of the Bridge End Hotel, Newcastle, which led to binding money being deposited on the spot.

Stephen duly started his race on Saturday 23rd January 1869 and, sculling coolly and seemingly within himself, was leading by half a length after 300 yards when calamity struck his opponent. Boyd caught his left hand scull under a short piece of floating timber and then lost the scull altogether and capsized. Fortunately he was able to get a leg across the upturned hull before he was rescued by some youths in a sculler boat, but the race was lost. Stephen was left to row over and collect the stakes. He had looked impressive but he had not been seriously tested.

Two days later, on Monday 25th January, James Renforth and James Taylor took on Matthew Scott and Andrew Thompson over the Champion course – the High Level Bridge to the Scotswood Suspension Bridge – a distance of about three and a half miles. Betting was heavy, mostly at even money, although a short time before the start, the 'big 'uns', Scott and Thompson were 11 to 10 on before dropping back to evens after an unconvincing warm-up on the river.

After a frantic start, Renforth and Taylor settled to their work, and, rowing beautifully together began to draw away from their heavier opponents who seemed unable to apply their undoubted power evenly. The *Robert Chambers* seemed to fly across the surface of the water and by the time the crews reached the new, partially constructed Redheugh Bridge, a distance of about 500 yards, Renforth and Taylor had a lead of three lengths. From hereon in the race became a procession, with Renforth and Taylor easing as they pleased and taking time to wave to their cheering supporters ranged along the north bank of the Tyne as they made their triumphant way up river. Despite this they were at one point 200 yards in the lead and they eased again before a final sprint brought victory by eight lengths, about 90 yards. The time from bridge to bridge was 22 minutes and 30 seconds and the collection for the beaten crew, who had continued to row doggedly if erratically, realised a handsome £6 10s.

Two significant factors were apparent in the crushing victory of Renforth and Taylor. Firstly, the quickness, lightness and elasticity of their stroke, described by the *Newcastle Daily Chronicle* as 'peculiarly their own', which surely shows that Taylor had adopted the low position, powerful leg drive, and bottom sliding technique of his stroke man. It certainly led the *Chronicle* journalist to comment that he believed their stroke would make them almost invincible. Secondly, as well as their supremely effective stroke, they had benefited from near-perfect steering because James Taylor had adopted a foot-operated rudder which he worked from the bow seat. No doubt he had taken advantage of observing the St John four's foot operated rudder at the Paris Regatta of 1867, but foot steering would be an important feature of Tyne rowing from now on.

It had been planned to follow the pair race with a contest in fours, with each pair selecting two more men to take part, but, unsurprisingly in the light of their heavy defeat, Scott and Thompson were not keen to participate in another race so soon. A challenge issued to Scott and Thompson on February 3rd 1869 by James Taylor, James Renforth, William Matfin and Thomas Matfin received no response. Renforth wanted to remain active, but finding a suitable sculling opponent was proving impossible and it looked increasingly unlikely that a pair-oar or even a four-oar match could be arranged. For the moment James had to be content with coaching other rowers, refereeing contests and acting on behalf of other professionals.

He was still immensely popular with both his backers and the general public and could count on a good reception wherever he went on Tyneside. The Cash Book of Tynemouth Amateur Rowing Club shows two payments late in 1868; one of £6 7s 0d for 'Renforth's Medal' and another of £5 15s 0d for 'Garland (Renforth's Medal)'and he received other valuable gifts to mark his championship triumph. A gossip columnist on the *Gateshead Observer*, a paper which was certainly more interested in Renforth's position within his own community than any other, described him in February 1869 as 'living like a king' since attaining the championship. Rings, cigar and pipe cases, and medals were presented and, perhaps giving more insight into the relationship between a sculler and his backers, an inscribed gold watch and massive Albert chain worth 25 guineas. This was presented at a testimonial dinner held at the Trafalgar Inn (James

*The Championship course and the King's Meadows islands c.1860.*

Taylor's public house) with the newspaper report saying that the watch had been promised by Renforth's backers if he should win the race against Kelly.

The high life James was leading resulted in an alarming expansion of his waistline. When a double scull match was proposed – Taylor and Renforth against James Percy and Mark Addy – Renforth wanted five weeks to prepare as he was said to need to lose 14 lbs before he was fit to row. The match never took place. Henceforth Renforth always needed time to shed weight before a big race and, when he sometimes competed in minor contests without training sufficiently hard, he was liable to 'blow up' if pushed hard.

At the start of the summer Renforth was engaged at a wage of £1 10s a week to coach the gentlemen of Tynemouth Amateur Rowing Club. The club cashbook records that he was paid £3 fortnightly and appears to have carried out his duties as coach from May 15th 1869 for four weeks. Thirty shillings a week was a good wage, since a shipyard rivetter, a skilled man, might expect to receive 25 shillings for a full week's work. Renforth was not coaching full time but was receiving more than a shipyard tradesman. It is interesting to see in the same cashbook that, later in the summer, James Taylor is receiving the same rate as the champion.

A few days before he began coaching for Tynemouth, Renforth is found acting for Joseph Sadler, one of the London professionals, in trying to arrange a match on the Tyne with James Percy for £200 a-side. From being a relatively unknown sculler 12 months previously, Renforth had become a respected member of the professional rowing fraternity, entrusted to act as coach, referee and agent – even by the Thames men.

He must have felt that he could no longer fulfil his duties as a militiaman because he is recorded as having deserted from the Durham Royal Garrison Artillery on the 5th May 1869, when he would have had about a year left to serve. The regiment can not have been too bothered about his desertion. Renforth would have been very easy to find, but one can only speculate as to what the sporting public would have done if he had been arrested just prior to an eagerly awaited race on the Tyne. One suspects that a blind eye was turned to his absence.

Renforth now responded to a challenge from the Hickey brothers of Australia, offering a single scull race or a pair-oar contest against Renforth and James Taylor, but this challenge also came to nothing. Setting up rowing races across the globe presented formidable logistical problems, with long sea passages to take into account, but Renforth's greatest difficulty was that no serious backer fancied the chances of any other sculler in a straight forward race with the champion.

Renforth had to fall back on a novelty race to keep him occupied on the water. While he was coaching the Tynemouth Amateurs, James Taylor was doing the same for the Tyne Amateur Rowing Club members. Friendly rivalry between the two training groups led to a challenge being issued for a pro-am pair-oar race. A few years on and nothing like this would have been considered, but in 1869 professional and amateur rowing coexisted happily on the Tyne, and although there was some discussion of the propriety of the contest, it was decided to proceed.

The race was to be over a two mile course – from the High Level Bridge to the Meadows Public House – Mr James Wallace (stroke) and James Taylor competing against James Renforth (stroke) and Mr G.S. Gulston. Wallace was a well known Tyne amateur who often acted as referee in professional matches, while Gulston, who was newly arrived in the North East, was the brother of the captain of the London Amateur Rowing Club. The prize was to be a gold medal for the professional in the winning boat. Wallace and Taylor had use of the champion pair *Robert Chambers*,

*Joseph Sadler, 1871 – The Thames oarsman who joined the Winship crew in 1871 and made the trip to Canada. Sadler and Renforth enjoyed friendly relations, with Renforth acting as Sadler's agent on Tyneside in 1869. After Renforth's death Sadler became champion sculler.*

which indicates that, despite Renforth's status as champion and stroke of their partnership, Taylor was undoubtedly still the boss. Renforth and Gulston rowed in the *Lord Durham*.

The race took place at 7pm on Monday 31st May 1869, which, with work having finished for the day, ensured a good crowd. Betting started at evens, but when Renforth and Gulston appeared rowing unsteadily, it soon switched to 2 to 1 on Wallace and Taylor, and stayed at 2 to 1 on despite Renforth and Gulston winning the toss and choosing the inside station. The inability of Renforth and his amateur partner to row together proved to be their downfall.

They quickly dropped behind and every time Renforth tried to put on the power to cut the gap to the *Robert Chambers* he was too strong for Gulston and rowed the bow round to the south. Although Wallace's fitness was very suspect, Renforth and Gulston could not keep their boat straight enough to apply the necessary pressure and cause Wallace to crack. Incidentally this account shows that Renforth was stroking the boat on what we would call the 'bow' side. Evidence of contemporary models, illustrations, and race accounts such as this show that boats were commonly rigged with the stroke oar on the 'bow' side.

Despite Renforth's best efforts, easing to allow the boat to straighten, rowing within himself most of the way, and offering his partner words of encouragement, Wallace and Taylor won easily in 12 minutes 35 seconds. Gulston would no doubt have felt bad about his inability to match his partner's strength but Renforth was enormously powerful and throughout his career even the professionals found it difficult to match up to him in a pair.

After failing earlier in the year to persuade Mark Addy and James Percy to take them on in a double scull, Renforth and Taylor now tried to set up a pair-oar race with the same duo. Percy responded – but only to demand that Renforth be debarred. Taylor swiftly agreed to the demand and promised to find another partner. As recognition of his great skill and power grew, James Renforth was to find it progressively harder to earn his living as a professional rower. His elder brother, Thomas, now took part in a pair-oar race on the Tyne for a small stake, and won easily, but this is a rare reference to Thomas as an oarsman. He was certainly third in rank behind James and Stephen among the Renforth boys.

James went off to King's Lynn Regatta – by steamer to Hull and then on by train – to take part in the scullers' race. Mark Addy withdrew and although Joseph Sadler raced, he was far from fit and Renforth won easily.

Less than a week later Renforth was debarred from the Aire Stakes, the scullers championship of the Leeds Regatta, which he had won in 1868. The response of the

Tyne Champion Four, whoever they might be at the time, was to declare their intent not to compete at Leeds. However life never seemed to be dull for James Renforth. On Sunday 10th June he was sculling at top speed in the skiff *Adelaide* alongside the Meadows, when he was in collision with an open boat going the other way. The open boat weighed almost three times as much as the skiff and Renforth was lucky to escape with a broken washboard and breakwater. As the bow of the open boat rode up over the lower slung *Adelaide* it scraped the skin off Renforth's side but fortunately he was not seriously injured.

The regatta season was now in full swing and Renforth competed next at Hull and then at Durham. Renforth and Taylor lost the coxed pairs race at Hull and were beaten on a foul by the local pairing of Newby and Marshall at Durham.

James Renforth does not seem to have been very fit at this time. He was no doubt enjoying his new life as a celebrity, and his lack of a serious match to look forward to would have made getting down to hard training an unattractive prospect. Another view might be that, since he was unable to get a good match as a sculler, even being debarred from the Aire Stakes at Leeds, and was also being debarred from pair oar contests, now was a good time to lose a few low value races to encourage the opposition. After their success in Durham, Newby and Marshall were certainly tempted by a challenge to meet Renforth and Taylor over a buoyed course on the Wear (the Wear at Durham was notorious for fouls caused by the narrow, winding nature of the river and the bloody-mindedness of the oarsmen).

Renforth moved on to the Hartlepools Regatta on Wednesday 14th July , and, in front of a dumbfounded crowd, was soundly beaten by the Gateshead veteran and old adversary, James Boyd. Difficult conditions, the less favoured station, and a boat which was not suitable for the chop that had been raised, contributed to Renforth's defeat, but suspicions were aroused nonetheless. I reproduce the report from the *South Durham Herald* of Saturday 17th July 1869 as it captures the full flavour of the champion's appearance at a small, recently instituted regatta.

**On Wednesday last, this regatta – which in the interests of one of our most popular and healthy of athletic sports, should be placed on such a basis to render it an annual event – took place on the Hartlepool Slake. The weather was, unfortunately, somewhat unfavourable – indeed, out of compliment, perhaps to the regatta, it assumed an 'aquatic' character – rain falling just before the commencement of proceedings, and clouds threatening throughout them. A large company assembled on the rough glacis or embankment surrounding the broad sheet of water called the Slake; and on the committee's barge – a commodious structure, gay with bunting, and provided with a temporary 'saloon,' in charge of mine host**

of the Raglan Hotel – a goodly array of lady visitors took up positions of vantage, and regarded with great interest the lively proceedings of the day. One of the chief attractions was the appearance of the renowned Tyneside oarsman, James Renforth, champion of England, and therefore, we may almost say, of the world. Wherever this redoubtable sculler went, he was followed by an admiring crowd that watched him and his boat with unflagging attention; and when he stepped into the skiff preparatory to the contest in which he was engaged, a buzz of admiration greeted the sight of his gigantic biceps, on the ropy and swelling surface of which was a tatooed design of a striking character. The champion, however, looked rather too large, and as though he had been neglectful of his preparation. Still, offers to back him at almost any price were freely made, and as freely left without response. It appeared that, as we understood, the skiff in which Boyd was to row had 'happened an accident' through being carelessly placed on some railway trucks or waggons, one of which tilted over and smashed in the boat's bow; and as neither Taylor (Tyne) nor W. Nicholson and Gillander (Tees men) put in an appearance, it was left to James Boyd (Tyne) to row against the champion in a short skiff belonging to the Neptune Amateur Rowing Club. This seemed to render Renforth's victory still more assured; and when, at the start, the champion went away with the lead, the affair was looked upon as all but over. Some astonishment, however, prevailed when it was observed that Boyd, with the advantage of the best, or windward station, was actually gaining on the champion; and astonishment gave way to bewilderment when, after the turn at the further end of the course, Renforth was plainly in difficulties, and making considerable leeway. Boyd came on from the turn, rowing a good, straight course, and rapidly leaving the champion behind, till, when he reached the finish, he was in advance by any number of lengths under thirty. A dead silence prevailed as the spectators saw this extraordinary result of a match that was called a race and looked like a friendly arrangement; and, presently, statements of a very unflattering character to Renforth were freely indulged in. We may, however, mention that the conqueror of Harry Kelley had the worst station, and that it was a losing station for competitors throughout the day. Still, it was difficult to conceive that Boyd could have won on his merits, although he is a pretty, powerful sculler, with plenty of dash and stamina combined.

Renforth and Taylor needed to sort out the four oar situation in order to send a crew to the prestigious and lucrative Thames Regatta and Renforth also had to get fit if he was to defend his title of Champion of the Thames which he had won at the regatta the previous year. Moreover Renforth had shown no signs of being able to combine the roles of celebrity and super-fit athlete. On the contrary, at the events to which he travelled, he was increasingly becoming remarkable for the size of his stomach. He had to find a satisfactory niche in society which would also allow him to train and to race.

In mid-June Renforth and Taylor settled their differences with two former members of the Champion Four, Matthew Scott and Robert Chambers. Taylor presented a financial statement which satisfied Chambers and Scott, and the four oarsmen parted on friendly terms. This left Taylor and Renforth free to recruit for their proposed four without the possibility of acrimonious exchanges with previous incumbents. At around the same time, or at any rate by the beginning of August, Renforth became landlord of the Belted Will Inn, off the Scotswood Road.

It was a career route which had been tried and had failed with a number of rowers – Harry Clasper probably being the most notable – but despite 'Elswick's' efforts to create a Championship of the Tyne in order that Renforth would not have to enter the licensed trade, inevitably, it seemed, that is where he ended up. Renforth could now look forward to a new phase of his career – on land as a publican and on the river as the next stroke of the Tyne Champion Four. The unwillingness of single scullers and their backers, and now even pairs, to take him on in a straight forward race had forced him to change the focus of his efforts on the water. He would need to concentrate on stroking the four and encouraging customers to drink in his pub if he was to continue to make a living out of professional rowing.

# Stroking the Champion Four – 1869

Three weeks into July and the *Chronicle*'s aquatics correspondent was looking forward to the Thames Regatta, and not mincing his words!

**'Renforth, knowing well the vast amount of superfluous flesh he will have to get rid of before he is fit, has taken plenty of hard work on the river, and has now succeeded in reducing himself to about 11 stone'**

*Newcastle Daily Chronicle* Saturday July 24th 1869

Two Tyne four-oar crews had gone into training. One was an experienced crew that Thomas Matfin had gathered around himself, made up of Tom Matfin (stroke), William Matfin, Andrew Thompson, and James Boyd. In the other four, Taylor and Renforth had taken the bold step of recruiting two members of the Pelaw Main Trimmers crew – John Martin and Thomas Heron. At one point the Matfins had seemed likely to throw their lot in with Taylor and Renforth, but in the event two different fours had emerged.

Rowing was a tremendously popular sport with working men at this time and groups of work mates would combine to race against each other. In most cases the challenge, for a small stake, would be made over a pint and no record of the contest has come down to us. However there are sufficient printed challenges appearing in the *Chronicle*, which cost hard-earned money to have inserted, to show that there were some very serious working men's crews about.

> The Gallowgate skinners, hearing that the Blaydon skinners wish to row them a four-oared match, the Gallowgate skinners are willing to g.ve them a tussle for their own stake. Or R. Armstrong will row any of the Blaydon crew in open boats; or E. Lee will row any of the above crews in skiffs. Either of the above matches can be made this evening at the house of H. Barlow, Cumberland Arms, for £5 or £10 a-side.

Newcastle Daily Chronicle *September 28th* 1868

There are challenges and race reports featuring drapers, skinners, carpenters, smiths, tailors, trimmers, grocers, theatre supers (supernumerary actors), butchers, shoemakers and even barristers (although that was in Durham during the Assizes) and

*Trimmers with their heart-shaped shovels. These men are at Blyth c.1900.*

this is by no means a comprehensive list. Pelaw Main was a place on the south bank of the river Tyne just east of Gateshead and trimming was a trade which was vital for the safe shipping of coal away from the Tyne. As the coal arrived from the collieries and was deposited in the hold as a pinnacled heap, gangs of trimmers spread it out evenly with large, heart-shaped shovels so that it would not shift when the ship was on passage. The Pelaw Main trimmers had become an extremely successful crew, defeating all comers among the Tyneside trades, and one suspects that Taylor had seized this opportunity to introduce fresh blood onto the Tyneside professional rowing scene. No doubt he also hoped that, since they would be grateful to him for giving them their chance, they might make a less argumentative 'engine room' than the previous occupants of the midships seats.

Renforth was promoted to stroke and Taylor reverted to his favoured bow seat once more. While Renforth continued to train hard he again tried to set up an international sculling match, this time with the American, Walter Brown. A pair oar challenge also went out to the Calderheads of Greenock, on the Clyde, who had beaten Taylor and Renforth at the Hull Regatta. Thomas Heron obviously did not develop into the oarsman it had been hoped he would and Thomas Winship of the well-known Tyne rowing family was brought into the boat to replace him.

Renforth and his companions visited the Chester Regatta at the beginning of August, where James won the sculling race as he pleased, and, with his team mates, also took the Watermen's Fours easily, which was worth £40. Renforth was now fully fit and a formidable stroke man – powerful, indefatigable and a good tactician. At Chester he had held his crew just behind the Manchester men before calling for an effort and shooting past their opponents.

Taylor and Renforth then graced the Wear Boat Club Regatta, winning the pair race (£5), in which they spurted, not because it was required to defeat the opposition, but to please the crowd. Renforth also won the skiff race (£8). Thirteen pounds was not a big pay day, but Sunderland was close by and the pair had their public – and also their public houses to consider. Taylor had been landlord of the Trafalgar Inn, New Bridge Street, Newcastle for some time but as the new holder of the licence at the Belted Will Inn, Hinde Street, Scotswood Road, Renforth was a novice publican. As mine host of a sporting house he needed to be behind the bar as much as possible. Supporters of aquatics – rowing fans to you and me – would then feel encouraged to come in and talk with the champion, and hopefully, quaff a good few pints of ale as well.

In practice this does not always work out as it should. Thirty years ago, when foot-ballers did not enjoy god-like status, or other-worldly wages, I remember going into a small pub in my home town of Gillingham, Kent, where the landlord, Jack Beby, had at one time been goalkeeper of the town's football team. Jack and I got talking – he had also played cricket in a works team alongside my father – and all his old photographs came out. He was a courteous and hospitable man and despite my protestations insist-ed on buying three of the five pints of beer which I drank through the evening. And I was the only customer in the bar that night! I left having enjoyed a wonderful evening in his company, but worrying that his skills as a publican nowhere approached those he had shown as a goalkeeper.

Renforth was doing less training for the sculls than usual although he would be taking part in the Thames race. The rules of the Regatta meant that he could only compete in two of the three professional rowing events so he withdrew from the pair, with Winship taking his place in the boat with Taylor.

Renforth duly won the sculls and Thomas Winship and James Taylor won the pairs. However disaster struck in the heats of the fours when Renforth's men were nar-rowly beaten into second place by the Surbiton crew, with Matfin's crew (also from the Tyne) third. The defeat was blamed on poor steering by the cox but, as events unfolded through the rest of the year, it may be looked upon as a stroke of fortune. Failure to win on the Thames was to lead to a high stakes 'home and home' match later in the year. The Tyne men returned home, having been unable to repeat the feat of 1868, when they whitewashed the Cocknies, but eager to get their revenge for defeat in the fours.

Renforth's proposed match with Walter Brown now fell through. Brown did not want to row on the Tyne – he preferred the Thames – and although Renforth would have been happy to face Brown on the London river, his backers thought otherwise. It must have been intensely frustrating for James – knowing that he could destroy any sculler in the world but unable to secure a single match.

Younger brother Stephen was due to race over two miles against Hugh Minnigan for £20 and the final deposit of £5 a-side had to be made at the Belted Will Inn, James's pub, on Friday 3rd September 1869. This was another ploy to bring in the punters, who would attend to see the money 'planked', listen to the chaff, and perhaps even have a bet themselves. James, as well as being his brother's coach, lent Stephen his fine skiff *Adelaide* to take part in the race. Stephen started favourite at 5 to 4 on.

James piloted his brother up river from the paddle box of the referee's boat, but despite the fine skiff and the top class coaching, Stephen lost. He had got caught up with the river dredger – a frequent hazard during races on the Tyne – but he also was not fit enough to make up the ground after the mishap. This was the moment when what had seemed a promising sculling career tailed off. Stephen would never approach the achievements of his illustrious brother, although he later became famous for diving into the Tyne at the drop of a hat to rescue any unfortunate who had got into difficulties in the river.

Meanwhile further challenges were winging their way round the country as the various fours tried to sort out which of them was really the best. Patchy results during the regatta season had left all the crews fancying their chances in matches against their rivals. Some commanded more respect than others and when the Cartsdyke crew suggested rowing a race in 20 ft jolly boats, James Renforth poured scorn on their proposal.

> THE TYNE CREW V. THE CLYDE CREW.—James Renforth, the champion, requests us to state in reply to the communication from the Cartsdyke worthies that he considers his men men, and not children, as boats twenty feet long are only intended for four small boys. He (Renforth) wishing, however, to give the " worthies" a trial of their skill, will row the four of them single matches, one after the other, on the same day, in best and best boats 20 feet long, for their own sums.

Newcastle Daily Chronicle, *Friday 17th September 1869.*

*David Clasper*

*John Bright, who was awarded victory by the referee after a bad-tempered, fouling, open boat match with Renforth in October 1869.*

Eventually a 'home and home' contest, one race on the Thames and one on the Tyne, was arranged with the Surbiton crew. Each race was to be for £200 a-side. Renforth had also finally managed to find himself an opponent, but was engaged at a huge disadvantage. He was to take on John Bright, the renowned Tyne open boat rower, in open boats, from the High Level Bridge to the Meadows House, 1³/₄ miles for £100. The real sting, however, was that Bright was to get two lengths at the start. Overhauling Bright without incurring a foul would be a near to impossible task. For whatever reason – perhaps he was desperate to race, or maybe he thought he could row right round Bright – Renforth agreed to those conditions. £50 a-side was not a huge sum for a race featuring the champion, so maybe he thought it was worth a gamble just to get out on the river in a single-scull again.

Around mid-September Renforth and Taylor went to Morpeth for a few days to relax before getting into hard training for the Bright race and the forthcoming contests against the Surbiton four. Renforth was certainly going to be busy over the next two months. Two weeks before his race with Bright Renforth wanted to take part in a swimming race at the Northumberland Baths, Newcastle, competing for a gold Maltese cross, but his backers declined to allow him to compete.

*The Star Hotel on Northumberland Street, Newcastle, where Renforth became involved in a dispute in October 1869. Renforth suffered an epileptic fit and had to be taken home in a cab.*

As the match against Bright approached, Renforth was said to be 'a little light' – a rare occurrence indeed! He was also praised by the *Chronicle* for attending Harry Clasper's rowing handicap as a spectator. James had a sense of history, and this is not the only occasion on which he would show respect for a veteran oarsman or the customs of the river.

Despite the two lengths start Bright was getting, Renforth was in demand at 5 to 2 on. Renforth had beaten Bright easily over the same course and distance, in Bright's favourite open boats on 28th March 1868, but the current match had been made because Bright's backers felt that he had progressed a great deal since then – and he did have a two lengths start.

A huge crowd was present to watch the two Tyneside favourites – many large factories closing down because their workers had taken themselves off to watch the race. Unfortunately the race itself was a bad-tempered, fouling affair, and although Renforth was first across the line, the referee, James Wallace, decided that Bright and Renforth should row over the next afternoon.

The row over the following day, the 6th October 1869, was just as bad. Although Renforth could row up to, and even get past Bright, he was unable to quit him completely and once again a series of fouls occurred. Renforth got to the finish first again, but on this occasion James Wallace decided that Renforth was to blame and gave the race to Bright. Renforth must have regretted ever agreeing to the conditions of this race and certainly from now on, if an opponent asked for a handicap, he always insisted on a level start with the handicap being taken at the finish. A challenge to Bright to row again, with Renforth's backers putting up £300 to Bright's £100, on the condition that both men kept to their own sides was declined. Bright knew who was the better man and that, in a straight forward race, even with a two lengths start, he would lose.

It had been a bad two days for Renforth, brought to a sour and alarming conclusion by an abusive customer who harangued James while he was having a drink with James Taylor in the Star Hotel, Northumberland Street. Upset and under stress, he dropped down in an epileptic fit. He was taken home in a cab and attended to by a doctor.

The most interesting event of the entire two days was the sudden appearance, shortly after the end of the race on the first day, of a very rare sight indeed on the Tyne, a female skiff rower. Here is the report of the shocked *Chronicle* journalist from the newspaper of 6th October 1869.

A FEMALE SKIFF ROWER.—Yesterday afternoon, strong evidence was given of the universal passion felt in the North for aquatic pursuits. About half-past four o'clock, the passengers over the temporary bridge across the Tyne were astonished to see a female making her way up the river in a skiff. The craft was one of the long fine skiffs frequently used in racing, and the brave female rower sat it with considerable confidence. She pulled with the skill of an adept at the art, and feathered her oar in capital style. Of course the appearance of so strange an aspirant for aquatic fame attracted considerable atention, and as she entered underneath one arch of the bridge there was a rush on the part of the onlookers to the other side of the roadway to witness her emerge. The lady, however, proved that in addition to her rowing ability she was possessed of a certain amount of smartness, which she used after going part of the distance through the arch in backing the skiff, and before the spectators were aware of the fact was some distance down the river.

Controversy over the race with Bright continued, with letters appearing in the columns of the *Chronicle* proposing reforms to the rules of boat racing. Most correspondents thought the obvious solution was for men to stick to their own sides – and on that note the Editor declared the matter closed.

As for the upcoming matches against the Thames, both crews had agreed to use coxswains and Renforth was pleased to obtain the services of Thomas Wilson, a youth of 15, who was so small he weighed only three stones 11 pounds – which sounds frightening. However we should not forget that the poor social conditions which prevailed meant that it was probably not difficult to find a boy whose growth had been stunted by long periods of malnourishment. The trick was in finding one whose mind had not been enfeebled by the poor diet: a boy who could take instructions and steer the boat under conditions of great stress and excitement. There was a tendency to seek out the smallest youth possible: the articles stated that

*Robert Clasper aged 11. He successfully coxed Harry Clasper's crew in 1859.*

boats should carry bona fide coxswains, to prevent the carrying of a tiny child as supercargo, and earlier in the negotiations of the agreement the Tyne men had tried to stipulate a minimum weight for the cox of five stone. Having secured the services of a boy weighing considerably less than that, they were no doubt pleased that they had not insisted on the weight limit.

The colours of the Tyne crew had been chosen by James Taylor. The handkerchief was white with a deep blue border, the Newcastle coat of arms filling in the four corners. In the centre the portraits and the names of the men and the coxswain surmounted the figures '1869'.

The four, James Renforth (stroke), John Martin (3), Thomas Winship (2), James Taylor (bow), trained on the Tyne until Thursday October 28th 1869, when they boarded the 7.15am train to London. They took with them the *Tyne*, a very fine new boat built especially for these races by Robert Jewitt of Dunston. The *Tyne* was very lightly built and on arrival in London many observers considered the northern crew to be 'under-boated' – that is their boat was too small to carry the weight of the crew and lacking in the necessary stiffness to carry her way through waves.

Dimensions of the *Tyne* were as follows:

| | |
|---|---|
| Length | 42 feet |
| Breadth amidships | 19 inches |
| Height at stem | $7^{1}/_{4}$ inches |
| Height at stern | $6^{1}/_{4}$ inches |
| Weight | 105 lbs |
| Construction | Cedar |

There was still some doubt as to how the Tyne four would perform. Early in their training it was noticeable to river watchers that John Martin, who sat behind Renforth, had a much more upright, less all-action style than the stroke oar, which made it difficult for both of them to row together. By the time the crew left for London, Martin had adapted to Renforth's low position and leg driving, sliding style, but it was still uncertain whether or not the crew could maintain their cohesion under pressure in a race. Martin was a novice professional, very little known, even in the North, and he had been forced to ease his training on the Tyne when his buttocks had become blistered. Race rowing was a tough business in the days when seats remained fixed and it was the oarsmen's buttocks that slid across the wood!

The course was the traditional one, from Putney to Mortlake, still the course for the Oxford and Cambridge University boat race. The crews measured up as follows:

### TYNE FOUR

| | Age | Weight st lbs | Height ft ins |
|---|---|---|---|
| 1. James Taylor (bow) | 32 | 10 0 | 5 $7^{1}/_{2}$ |
| 2. Thomas Winship | 26 | 11 0 | 5 $7^{1}/_{2}$ |
| 3. John Martin | 26 | 11 8 | 5 $8^{1}/_{2}$ |
| 4. James Renforth (stroke) | 27 | 11 11 | 5 $7^{1}/_{2}$ |
| Thomas Wilson (cox) | 14 | 3 12 | |
| Total years | 125 | Total weight 48 stones 3 lbs. | |

### THAMES FOUR

| | Age | Weight st lbs | Height ft ins |
|---|---|---|---|
| 1. Joseph. H. Sadler (bow) | 29 | 11 0 | 5 $9^{1}/_{2}$ |
| 2. Henry Kelley | 38 | 10 12 | 5 $8^{1}/_{2}$ |
| 3. William Messenger | 19 | 11 8 | 5 10 |

| 4. George Hammerton (stroke) | 32 | 10 7 | 5 7 |
| G.W. Hammerton (cox) | 10 | 3 10 | |
| Total years | 128 | Total weight 47 stones 9 lbs. | |

The race took place on the November 5th and northern supporters heading for the river were fair game for London children collecting pennies for their guys. Or as the *Chronicle* put it, 'and the smart youths busy collecting contributions from the passers by did not fail to levy black mail upon such evident countrymen as the northern contingent'!

Leading up to the race the Thames men had been favourites, but at the start bets were being made at even money. The Tyne crew rowed stripped to the waist, as was their custom, while the Londoners kept their white rowing jerseys on.

The Thames crew won the toss and elected to start from the Middlesex station. Both crews got away cleanly, with the Thames four rating 42 strokes to the minute and the Tyne men rating 41. After 100 yards the *Tyne* was one third of a length ahead and Renforth, confident that the race was under control, called out, 'Long'. The Tyne crew dropped its rate to a steady 38 strokes to the minute. By Craven Cottages they were clear and after a mile they were $2^{1/2}$ lengths up. The Thames crew was not evenly balanced between the bow and stroke sides, which made steering difficult for the cox. Even at this early stage it was clear that, barring a mishap to the Tyne men, the Londoners were beaten. Renforth revelled in this position of dominance – and gave what was already becoming a characteristic gesture of triumph.

**At times Renforth would hold up his hand and give it a triumphant swing, one or two of his oarsmen now and then joining in the diversion.**

*Newcastle Daily Chronicle* 6th November 1869

The Tyne crew won by about 80 yards, finishing fresh and rowing well within themselves. Distance from Putney to Mortlake, 4 miles 3 furlongs. Time 20 minutes 30 seconds. All of the Tyne men, and their young coxswain, had acquitted themselves well, but the *Chronicle* had this to say about Renforth:

**Renforth will henceforth become as celebrated as a stroke oar as he has hitherto been as a sculler. The presence in the boat of such a leader is in itself a strong earnest of success. The confidence, earnestness, and high spirits of the man are quite infectious, and it would indeed be a moderate crew that was not inspired to do its very utmost by the force of his example.**

*Newcastle Daily Chronicle*, 6th November 1869

*The river at Scotswood with rowers, mid-19th century.*

Now the four had to be ready to take the Thames men on again in 13 days on the Tyne. Arriving back in Newcastle on Saturday night they took a few days off before resuming training on Tuesday 9th November. The next race was due to take place on Thursday 18th November. Renforth and Taylor were also now engaged to race in a double scull against Henry Kelley and Joseph Sadler for £200 two days after the fours race. Double scull racing was something of a Thames speciality and the race seems to have been arranged to offer the Londoners some hope of reward for undertaking the trip north. They were very much the underdogs in the fours after taking such a comprehensive beating on their home river. However they quickly set about trying to remedy what they saw as the two major problems which had led to their defeat on the Thames.

First, they rearranged the crew in order to improve the bow side-stroke side balance. Harry Kelley took the stroke seat, with Joseph Sadler at 3, Messenger at 2 and George Hammerton rowing bow. Secondly, the London-built boat they had used on the Thames had weighed 147 lbs, 42 lbs more than that of the Tyne men. Now the Londoners appealed for one of the Northern Clubs to lend them a suitable boat and the Wear Boating Club obliged. This was another Jewitt-built craft, at 119 lbs still slightly heavier than the *Tyne*, but a huge improvement on their previous boat. After two outings in the Wear boat they determined to use it in the race. They also, without comment, had changed their cox!

The race took place into the teeth of a westerly gale and Kelley's crew were delighted when they won the toss and were able to choose the northern station. They would be able to tuck in close to the river bank in the early stages and thus have the most sheltered of the water. Unusually the start was not from the second arch of the High Level Bridge but out in the river opposite the Old Mansion House. Both crews stripped this time, despite the cold conditions, although the Londoners decided to retain their caps.

After a clean start the Londoners drove ahead, taking advantage of their slightly more sheltered station and rating 44 strokes to the minute. Two hundred yards into the race they were half a length ahead, but Renforth was content to bide his time.

At the Skinner Burn the Londoners eased back slightly and the northern crew, seeing its opportunity, and putting on the power, drew level. The gale was now at its height, and in the rough water which was their lot Renforth's crew could not pull through their opponents. Renforth called for even greater efforts and, labouring through the chop, the Tyne boat went a length up at the head of the Grindstone Quay. Eventually the *Tyne* was able to get clear water and move over to the north and hug the shore. Once inside the Annie islet, the coxswain, Wilson, used a large sponge (which he pitched overboard once it was saturated) and a tin pan to bail out the water the *Tyne* had shipped in the difficult conditions. Renforth and his crew retained control for the rest of the race and passed under the Scotswood Bridge three lengths ahead to a salvo of small arms fire from the Scotswood Paper Mill.

That night the whole Tyne crew appeared on stage, in aquatic costume, at the Tyne Theatre. They made their entrance in the final scene of the comic operetta *The Waterman* and received prolonged and rapturous applause. Also on the bill was Professor Beckwith, champion swimmer of the world, with his pupil, 'The Man Fish', who performed extraordinary feats in an onstage aquarium!

In what was a continuing feast of aquatics, Walter Brown, the American sculler, took on William Sadler on Friday. Brown, who had initially challenged Renforth, was quite content to pit himself against the lesser talent of the London sculler. Taylor and Renforth had helped Brown during his preparations on the Tyne, and Renforth had even lent him his skiff *Adelaide*, so he had a very fine craft in which to row. The American, who was as popular with the Tynesiders as they were with him, duly defeated Sadler.

Finally, on the Saturday, Renforth and Taylor raced against Joseph Sadler and Harry Kelley in a double sculls match. Taylor and Renforth were ill-suited to scull together. Taylor was accustomed to rowing 'right hand over left' and had to reverse his hands to accommodate Renforth. They also had problems with their boat and their oars, but despite all this the better prepared and skilful Londoners only defeated them by a length.

The following Tuesday, before they returned south, some of the London crew took the time to visit Walker Churchyard to look at Bob Chambers's monument.

For Renforth the rest of the year was taken up in a round of rowing club dinners and presentations – to Robert Jewitt for building the *Tyne* and to the coxswain Thomas Wilson for the straight course he steered during the races – with some helpful advice to young Thomas to keep his weight down if he wanted to continue to steer the Tyne four. Since Renforth was so often on the receiving end of criticism from the *Chronicle* about his weight he must surely have had a smile on his face when suggesting abstinence to the tiny cox! One would have

*David Clasper*

*The monument to Robert Chambers in Walker Parish Churchyard. The statue is now damaged.*

hoped that Renforth also tried to devote some time to his business at the Belted Will Inn, but, given how heavily engaged he had been on the water through the year, and the obvious demands for him to put in celebrity appearances, one doubts that he could have been assiduous in pursuing any other commercial goals.

As the rowing year came to an end, the usual challenges, and counter challenges, appeared in the *Newcastle Daily Chronicle*. Some were serious; some were speculative; some were, frankly, exotic: **A CHALLENGE FROM THE BISCAYAN FISHERMEN OF SPAIN.**

However on Wednesday November 3rd 1869 a challenge appeared from the St John crew in Canada. This was a group of fishermen from New Brunswick who had created a stir when they appeared in a foot steered coxless four at the Paris Regatta of 1867. They had won the amateur race against a background of concern as to whether or not they ought to have been classified as amateurs. The boat in which they rowed was much heavier than a Tyne racing shell, but against amateurs they had put up an impressive performance. They rowed at a very high rating, used no foot straps and had no buttons on their oars. The Tyne Champion Four, which included James Taylor, had also been in Paris in 1867 and had won the professional race and the prize of £100. Taylor therefore had had an opportunity to observe the St John crew first hand and perhaps saw a way to widen the horizons of the current Champion Four. He had quickly adopted the New Brunswickers' method of foot steering, but was probably less impressed with the heavy boat, the fast stroke and the lack of foot straps, or buttons on their oars. He would definitely have seen this as an excellent opportunity to make money out of a contest in Canada.

On Thursday 25th November 1869, the Tynesiders responded to the St John men with a proposal to race for £500 a-side over 4½ miles for the championship of the world. London and the men of the Thames had been conquered. The next step would be to meet the challenge from across the Atlantic.

## THE FORTHCOMING BOAT RACE.
### TO THE EDITOR OF THE DAILY CHRONICLE.

SIR,—It is to be hoped that whichever of the rival crews prove the best men in their home-and-home matches, which are at present causing so much interest in all parts of the kingdom, that a challenge be sent out to the celebrated Canadian rowers of St. John's, N.B. (the crew which easily beat the Oxford University and the London Rowing Club crews at the Paris International Regatta in 1867, and also the celebrated American crew of the Ward Brothers last November). They have proved themselves in all the matches first-class oarsmen, and have as yet been unconquered. Should a match be arranged between them, the greatest interest would be taken in it on both sides of the Atlantic. Should the Tyne crew prove the best, I believe they would be willing to row the Canadians without coxswains.—I remain, sir, yours respectfully, ARGUS.

30th October, 1869.

# The Transatlantic Challenge – 1870

Perhaps mindful of his brush with the law during the early days of 1869, Renforth started the new year quietly. His mentor, training partner and fellow member of the four, James Taylor, was trying to set up a race of his own with the temperamental Manchester sculler Mark Addy and was out training in a skiff. The weather in the early part of the year was poor and rowers were finding it difficult to get out on the river. James refereed an open boat race on the Tyne on January 29th in which the course had to be moved up river because of ice below Redheugh. There was continued optimism that the race against the St John crew might come off; and optimism turned to confidence when Renforth received two letters from Canada towards the end of February.

One was from St John, New Brunswick, setting out what course the proposed £1000 race would be rowed over. The St John crew wanted to row a six-mile race, rowing three miles to a fixed point, turning round it, and then rowing back to the start/finish. Turning in the middle of a race would be a new experience for the Tyne crew.

The other letter was from Montreal, from members of the recently formed Lachine Boating Club, who wanted to mark the opening of their clubhouse and grandstand with a contest between the two best crews in the world. They were willing to pay Renforth's crew £200 expenses to travel to Canada and race against the St John crew on their club course near Montreal. This injection of cash from a source external to the antagonists or their backers made the contest pretty well a certainty. Expenses were frequently squabbled over, even in matches between the Thames and the Tyne, so in any transatlantic tussle they were crucial. If the Lachine Boating Club members were as good as their word the Tyne four would definitely travel – although they would need to raise the stake of £500 and any additional expenses from the sporting Tyneside public. An appeal for backers went out from the *Newcastle Daily Chronicle*.

Renforth wrote back to Canada, accepting the challenge, although expressing some concerns over the control of spectators, the out and back course, and whether or not the course was subject to rough conditions. He was also concerned about possible accident or sickness in the crew. In the recent races against the Surbiton crew, only one member of each four had been named in the articles of agreement so that a substitute could be brought into the boat in case of illness or injury.

However, all was not well in Renforth's world. The *Newcastle Daily Chronicle* of Friday February 25th 1870, carried news of a change in his business activities.

JAMES RENFORTH, CHAMPION SCULLER OF ENGLAND. — The numerous friends of the worthy aquatic champion will be happy to hear that he has removed from his old premises in Scotswood Road to the Sir Charles Napier Inn, Queen Street, St. Nicholas' Buildings. Although the champion's new house is not exactly the sort of place we should like to see him in, yet it is centrally situated, and handy for his acquaintances resident on both sides of the Tyne. Renforth, we may add, appears determined to stick steadily to business, and callers at all reasonable hours may depend upon finding him at the bar, and upon enjoying, as well as the press of customers will allow, the pleasure of his society and conversation.

Exactly what lay behind Renforth's move is probably lost to us, but it is clear that the *Chronicle* journalist is concerned in some way about the transfer to the quayside. The champion had been landlord of the Belted Will Inn for less than a year before making this move. Today, Queen Street is the home of expensive restaurants and fashionable bars but one imagines that back in 1870, being adjacent to a busy trading quayside, one would get a good proportion of waterside low life frequenting the bar. And why not? Renforth was one of their own, and maybe it was pure snobbery on the part of the *Chronicle* writer which led him to express reservations about the Sir Charles Napier Inn. Some buildings in Queen Street were demolished to make way for the Tyne Bridge of 1929, and I believe that Renforth's former establishment was one of them. His first pub, the Belted Will Inn, Scotswood Road, has also been demolished.

Now Renforth began to work on the river with James Taylor in preparation for Taylor's match with Addy. The champion four also trained together, looking forward to their race in Canada which, at this time, they thought might happen as early as June. On the 1st March Renforth and Taylor attended the launch of new skiffs built for them by Robert Jewitt. Renforth's boat, *John Wilson Esq.*, (named after a North Shields merchant who had often put in stake money for Renforth) was a fine craft in the Jewitt tradition. Taylor's boat, the *Experiment* was built to a new design by a naval architect, Armstrong, who worked in Palmers Shipyard, Jarrow. The *Experiment* was round-hulled, with a keelson extending the full length of the craft to support the hull, which was at no point hollow in section. It also had steel rowlocks, which was unusual for the time. Most craft had wooden rowlocks set on iron outriggers as it was thought best to work the oar against wood. Renforth declared himself delighted with his craft, and although Taylor was satisfied with the *Experiment* he thought that some alterations would need to be made before the boat was fit to tackle rough water.

On Monday March 7th 1870 the Champion Four appeared on stage at the Tyne

Theatre, in aquatic costume, and in their boat! According to the publicity they were going to demonstrate the style with which they would beat the Canadians. It must have been a strange sight. One assumes that the boat must either have been faked or extremely well mounted to avoid sustaining damage during this bizarre exhibition of dry rowing.

Renforth was struggling with his weight again. Three weeks into March the *Chronicle* was worrying that he was very big and not rowing at his best, and that it would not do for him to be caught unprepared. The date of the contest with the St John crew was anything but certain. The Canadians wanted to row in August while the Tynesiders favoured June or September. Renforth continued to train in his skiff, and with the four, but the *Chronicle* still thought he was overweight.

A letter from Walter Brown was published in the rowing columns, describing Renforth as a friend, and giving some tips on the course at Lachine. Renforth, who had a reputation as a slow starter, tried to encourage an opponent by offering to race over a short course of a mile on the Tyne for £200 a-side. As an alternative he said that he would give six lengths at the finish to any man over four miles on the same river. Taylor should have raced against Addy on Monday May 16th, but Addy was unable to row because of a cut hand, so Taylor rowed over. Addy's stake was, of course, forfeit, but only in cases where the wager stated 'goes with the stakes' were side bets paid out.

Renforth was now matched with the ex-champion, Kelley, who had been on Tyneside racing, and beating, John Bright. The race was to take place at very short notice. Articles were drawn up at the initial meeting, and a date was set for only a week hence, over three miles, with Renforth's backers putting up £100 to Kelley's £80. Renforth was still not fit and must have thought better of taking on the tough Londoner because a few days later the *Chronicle*, the stakeholder, paid over £50 to Kelley, £10 of which had been put down on Renforth's behalf.

On June 4th Renforth was racing off scratch in James Taylor's Open Boat Handicap when he blew up completely and was defeated by the very moderate oarsman, Wilson ($2^{1/2}$ lengths), whom he should have disposed of easily. James was still really struggling to get fit even though the season was well advanced. There must have been some concern that his powers were on the wane, or that he could no longer be bothered to train as he should.

Professional and amateur rowing was now deep in the throes of a painful separation, nowhere more so than on the Tyne where the two codes had happily co-existed up to now. Amateur oarsmen were being ordered to leave the Albion and Northern Rowing Clubs, who counted among their members the top professional oarsmen in the North. Renforth was unable to make his customary trip to the King's Lynn Regatta because there was no longer a skiff race for professionals. On this matter the *Chronicle* was quite clear about where it stood:

> **We may mention that there was great dissatisfaction amongst spectators at the uninteresting nature of the programme, and it was the general opinion that if Cambridge is to be propitiated at the expense of the professional rowers, the regatta will fail.**

*Newcastle Daily Chronicle* Thursday June 9th 1870

The articles for the race in Canada were finally drawn up such that all could agree to them, and Renforth signed on behalf of the Tyne crew. The race would take place on Thursday September 17th 1870. Renforth was concerned that someone might try and 'nobble' the Englishmen before the race – Walter Brown had sent warnings about such things in a recent letter – and as well as signing the articles of agreement he wrote to the secretary of the Lachine Boating Club. James set out some of the precautions he would like taken to protect his men against interference. One concern was that they might be poisoned or doped and it was felt that the services of an English cook should be secured for the duration of their stay.

Renforth and Taylor were obliged to take a week out from training in June because it was Race Week on Newcastle's Town Moor and they both had marquees booked from which to dispense liquor and bonhomie. For a specimen like Renforth, who really did need hard training to keep him in shape, combining professional rowing with being a publican must have been extremely difficult. Nonetheless, soon after Race Week, the crew was established at the Ord Arms, Scotswood where the veteran Harry Clasper's dictum, 'the good old rule, the simple plan' and plenty of hard training was expected to deliver them fit and rowing well together before their departure for Canada.

In July, at the Durham Regatta, Renforth won the scullers' race, beating James Taylor. Later he led the four to victory, toying with the local heroes, the Marshalls, before leaving them in his wake. The *Tyne*, last year's wonder boat, was sold to a Hamburg rowing club at the Regatta, but the crew still awaited a new boat which Jewitt was building. In the meantime they borrowed a boat from Tynemouth Amateur Rowing Club (both Renforth and Taylor had coached them in the past year) in order to continue training. Unfortunately this boat did not 'run' well for them and they had to wait for the delivery of the new boat to make further progress. Renforth's bulk was again the subject of comment in the *Chronicle* and John Martin was also thought to be carrying too much condition.

On Tuesday July 12th Harry Clasper, one of the great heroes of the Tyneside rowing scene, died after a short illness. Only a few days before he had attended the

Durham Regatta. As well as being a fine sculler and stroke of a four, Harry had contributed hugely to the development of the racing shell. He always claimed to be the 'inventor of the present outrigger', which was his way of saying that he had taken an unworkable good idea and developed it until it did work. Harry Clasper was buried on Sunday July 17th with huge crowds gathering outside his home in Ouseburn on the morning of the funeral. Fittingly, the coffin was carried part of its way to Whickham, where Harry was to find his final resting place, by steamboat. Renforth and his crew were pall bearers along with members of two great Tyne rowing families, Thomas Taylor and Edward Winship.

Soon after Harry Clasper's funeral, James Taylor became ill. John Adams, a prominent backer of the four, took his place in the boat during training on the river, but was nowhere near fit enough to keep up with the rest of the crew. Fortunately James Taylor was soon well enough to resume training, but this incident pointed up the difficulty the Tyneside champions would face if one of their number fell ill in Canada. A professional crew required a professional spare man for emergencies if the stake money was not to be thrown away.

In the final week of July two new boats were launched which the Champion Four would take with them to Canada. Firstly, the *Jarrow-on-Tyne* took to the river from the slipway at Palmer's Shipyard, Jarrow. Built by Armstrong, the designer of Taylor's skiff, *The Experiment*, the *Jarrow* was, at 38 feet long and $21^1/_2$ inches in breadth, shorter and beamier than the boats they were accustomed to use for racing. But it was thought that the short, round-sectioned hull would turn well, a requirement of the forthcoming 'out and back' race, and also that it would ride over rough water. Two days later the *Dunston-on-Tyne* was launched from Robert Jewitt's Dunston boatyard. The *Dunston* was a typically fine-lined Jewitt craft, 43 feet long and $17^1/_2$ inches in breadth, which the crew expected to run best in smooth conditions. Since they could only rely on second-hand accounts of the course at Lachine, they needed to be ready for any type of water conditions that might occur. Renforth was also preparing to take two new skiffs with him to Canada. He was trying to set up a race against Henry Coulter of Pittsburgh, USA while he was in North America with the four.

The training was now beginning to taper off, since the four had achieved as much as they could in England, and would in any case have to bring themselves back to fitness after their Atlantic crossing. For their final public appearance on Tyneside the four joined the ex-rower, and now landlord of the Ravensworth Arms, Edward Winship (brother of Tom) on Newcastle's Town Moor for the Annual Military Review. Rowing enthusiasts and friends of the Champion Four were invited to partake of 'refreshments of first-rate quality' in the marquee and to bid farewell to their Tyneside heroes.

Champion crews could be expected to generate champion business. In contrast, at about the same time, reports were reaching the north that the historic Thames Regatta was experiencing financial difficulties. While Tyneside relaxed in the sure knowledge that it had become the world's premiere rowing centre, all was not well among the Cocknies.

The Champion crew departed from Newcastle Central Station at 6am on Monday August 8th 1870, and even at that hour 300 people gathered to give them a rousing send off.

It is rare that a first-hand account of the activities of professional rowers is found. Most rowers were poorly educated, and many, including Harry Clasper and James Renforth, had probably not attended school and thus had not been taught to read and write as boys. However, during the journey from Newcastle to Lachine, James Taylor kept a diary, which was published in the *Newcastle Daily Chronicle* of 7th September 1870. It is short, and to the point – the health and fitness of the crew is his greatest preoccupation – but full of practical observations,. It also gives an insight into attempts to train while on passage, and inevitably perhaps, documentary proof of James Renforth's ballooning weight!

*Newcastle Daily Chronicle* 7th September 1870

**LOG KEPT BY JAMES TAYLOR**

**Monday, August 8, 1870. – Left Newcastle at 6am. Had a pleasant trip to Glasgow, and stayed at the Union Hotel. Put boats and baggage on board the Hibernian.**

**Tuesday, August 9. – Sailed to Greenock, leaving Glasgow at 10 o'clock.**

**Wednesday, August 10. – Sailed from Greenock at three pm, and got a good cheer from all around. Lost sight of land in the middle watch. Weather very fine. The men commenced to exercise with dumb-bells, and also by picking up stones one yard apart as soon as we left the river. At 11 o'clock we all turned in.**

**Thursday, August 11. – There was some swell on, and two of the crew – Martin and Winship – were sick, but soon got better. In the afternoon we sighted a dis-abled steamship and took three passengers from her; and we had some fine fun afterwards with the porpoises following the ship. After tea we had more dumb-bell exercise, and picking up stones laid on the deck. The steamer we passed was the India of Glasgow, with 600 passengers for New York. She had broken some of her machinery, and had been five days at sea. Went to bed at 11 o'clock. All lights out at 11.38.**

Friday, August 12. – We are all well. Fine morning and calm weather; fair wind. Going eleven knots. Got on deck at seven o'clock. Had dumb-bell exercise till eight o'clock. Breakfast 8.30, lunch at twelve o'clock, dinner at four, tea at seven o'clock. Saw numbers of porpoises about the ship. We get good meat, and have a pleasant company of 60 saloon passengers, including both ladies and gentlemen. We had games at shuffle-board and quoits on deck, and after dark a game at cards. Fine weather, and vessel going 12 knots an hour. Got to bed at eleven o'clock.

Saturday, August 13. – On deck at seven am, and at once took dumb-bell and walking exercise, keeping at it for an hour. Strong S.S.W. Wind. We had a lottery at three o'clock for the nearest guess to the number of miles we had gone in 24 hours. The winner was 293. We have not seen a sail all day. To-night thick and foggy, but the crew are all well.

Sunday, August 14. – On deck at 7.30. Very foggy through the night, and continued throughout to-day. Going $10^1/_2$ knots. We had Church service on deck in the morning; captain officiated. We have a Catholic priest on board, and he took his people into the ladies cabin, and said mass. The ship is very steady, but the wind is northerly and cold. An excellent dinner was spread for us in the cabin. Reading and walking are all we have done to-day, in the shape of exercise.

Monday, August 15. – All well; on deck at 7.30; fine morning. We had dumb-bell and walking exercise until eight o'clock, when we took breakfast. Afterwards we inspected our boats, and found them all right; the passengers were much pleased with them. I sold a number of photographs of the crew to the passengers. The engineer took all of us through the engine-room in the afternoon. Going $10^1/_2$ knots, and fine weather. The steward has been very kind to us, and offered to cook anything special we required. We have been weighed to-day, with the following result:-

|  | st lb |  | st lb |
|---|---|---|---|
| Renforth | 12 2 | Winship | 11 2 |
| Martin | 12 6 | Taylor | 10 8 |

Had a grand concert at night, in the cabin. Went to bed at eleven o'clock.

Tuesday, August 16. – All well; on deck at 7.30. Very cold and wet, with head-wind. The vessel goes along very tidy, and she is a fine ship. The time with us is 9.45, and in England it is 12.45. Saw a ship to the north of us at ten o'clock, and saw more at 12 o'clock. Saw a large bottle-nosed whale. Had a lottery, 38 in, and

No. 277 won. It is still a head-wind, and the vessel is now pitching heavily. In the evening we had dumb-bell exercise. Winship is sick. We are now about a hundred miles from Newfoundland.

Wednesday, August 17. – Saw the land at 6.30 this morning, and glad of it. The ship had been pitching heavily all night, but we are all well. Went on shore to see St John's, Newfoundland. It is just like the Yorkshire coast outside, but the town itself is like a great fishing town; but it has a pretty little harbour. We got out our boat, and had a good row of about two miles in the harbour, but the weather was somewhat rough, and we had to make her go. The boat we took was the 'Jarrow'. The townspeople came in hundreds to the shore, and joined the passengers in giving us a hearty cheer. About 75 passengers leave us here; they are mostly Scotch tradesmen, settled in the place, and they come to England every year to buy clothing and other goods. We are busy unloading their traps as sharp as possible. We left St John's again at midnight, and steamed away across the waters on a beautiful moonlight night. We did not go to bed until one o'clock in the morning, being so calm and pleasant on deck.

Thursday, August 18. – Got on deck at 8 o'clock. Splendid weather, and the steamer going fast. Still running west, and just leaving the Banks of Newfoundland.

Friday, August 19. – All on deck at 7.30. We have had a stormy night, but the weather is better this morning. We are abreast of the Island St Paul, or the mouth of the gulf of St Lawrence, with a head wind blowing against us. We had breakfast, and then kept a smart look out for land; there were several small islands between, and one was covered with birds. To-day we had some good dumb-bell exercise. In the evening the weather became rather unpleasant, and we went to bed early.

Saturday, August 20. – All the crew well. We are now sailing into the mouth of the St Lawrence, with high hills covered with wood on one side. We reached Father Point and got pilot on board at six o'clock in the evening, and a pleasant night followed, with some good singing in the cabin, and a social glass of ale all round.

The four soon settled into their cottage by the St Lawrence river at Lachine, where they had engaged an English cook to guard against the possibility of interference with their food. Training began in earnest again immediately. They rose early, swam in the river, and then, well-wrapped up, undertook vigorous walking exercises on the roads near Lachine to try and sweat off excess flesh laid down during the sea voyage. The

*Chronicle* rowing correspondent – who uses no byline – but whom I know to have been a journalist by the name of Joseph Walton, was once again remarking on Renforth's and Martin's weight. 'Martin and Renforth, in particular, have become quite gross, and will require nothing short of severe work to bring them down to their racing weight.'

They had 26 days to get back to full fitness but after only two weeks of hard training each man was in racing trim and the crew was ready to take on the St John's men. Even Joseph Walton, seemingly satisfied now that Renforth's bulk was being reduced, was impressed with his enthusiasm for training: 'The champion in particular is full of vigour, and at times is like to pull the place down with the energy of his dumb-bell exercise.' (*Newcastle Daily Chronicle* Wednesday September 14th 1870)

Renforth, who already weighed in at 12 stone 2 pounds halfway through the Atlantic crossing, would have had to shed about a stone to get to his racing weight of around 11 stone 5 pounds. Meanwhile the plan to safeguard the men from poisoning, or other culinary skullduggery, had gone awry in a quite farcical manner. The English cook had gone missing along with a quantity of spirits from a decanter and as a result they had no food at all! She was dismissed that evening and from then on the crew took their meals at the nearby Lake View Hotel, where the wife of the proprietor was an Englishwoman of sober character.

Both the American and the Canadian newspapers were extremely interested in the Tynesiders, and the *Toronto Daily Globe*, in comparing the qualities of the opposing crews, expanded on what they considered was a big advantage which the St John crew, who made their living as fishermen and dockworkers, had over the Englishmen.

> A moral and physical advantage our own men have is due to their style of living. In England the custom obtains for all successful watermen to establish themselves as mine hosts of "The Ship," or "The Bells," or "The Star and Garter," where stakes are made for forthcoming events, racing matters are discussed over pewters and glasses, and other anti-condition proceedings are of daily and nightly occurrence. Then of a sudden mine host changes his character. A match has been made, and he rushes into training. Dieting and physicing, and old beer in place of loose living and brandy and water. So the system, to its inevitable injury, is kept alternating between the exactions of tavern keeping, and the rigour of severe training. In a six mile race, if a man has a weak spot in him, it is bound to come out. Our men will row to the end, because they are always "fit," as greyhounds for the leash.

*Reproduced in the* Newcastle Daily Chronicle *15th September 1870.*

The crew were less than flattered by this report and were most upset that anyone would think that they would adulterate drinking water with brandy, or maybe it was the other way round! Joseph Walton, as special correspondent, kept up the flow of information back to Tyneside. The newly laid Atlantic telegraph cable, which had been established as a reliable link in 1866, was expensive to use but provided previously unheard of immediacy for all those waiting for news back home. When Walton sent his report to Tyneside on the day after the race, it was the longest ever message sent from America to England by telegraph. Victorian journalists thought nothing of filing stories of many thousands of words and the less urgent and more comprehensive of his reports were sent by steam packet to Ireland and thence by telegraph. As well as writing about how training was going, which was important for Tyneside investors who might have contributed to the stake, and sent other sums out to be wagered in side bets, he provided an entertaining and varied account of the Tynesiders' stay in Canada and how the four were spending their time when they were not training. He wrote a long description of a visit to watch a game of Lacrosse played by Iroquois Indians. The women of the district also come in for some favourable and amusing comment. It appears that although well mannered, they were, by English standards, unreserved. Tom Winship, who was a bachelor, was the recipient of many direct personal questions, which had him blushing under the tan he had acquired on board ship. Having suffered as much embarrassment as he could bear, poor Tom had then to endure an equal amount of leg-pulling from his companions.

Both boats were used during practice on the course. The *Jarrow* was favoured when the water was rough, while the *Dunston* was kept for fine, smooth days. For some while the debate continued as to which boat should be used in the great race. James Taylor and John Adams strongly favoured the *Jarrow*, while Renforth was just as strongly impressed with the qualities of the *Dunston*. Finally the stroke man carried the day and the *Dunston* was selected and polished, ready for the race. *Jarrow* was also polished in case she should be needed.

Public interest in the race was enormous and the Englishmen received a constant stream of callers to their little cottage. Among the visitors were men from the Grand Trunk Railway workshops who had come to work in Canada from Northumberland and Durham. The unexpected presence of this body of supporters proved of the greatest service to the Tynesiders. The foot-steering apparatus of the *Dunston* was of faulty design and interfered with the bow man's ability to drive off the footboard as he should. James Taylor invented a semi-lunar lever, working freely on a pivot, which solved the problem. The new apparatus was quickly manufactured by the northcountrymen of the Grand Trunk Railway. They were also entrusted with adding eight inches

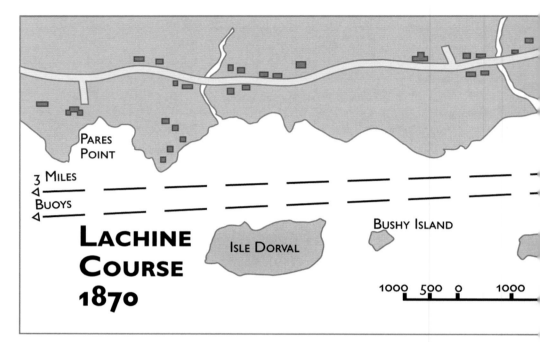

PARES
POINT

3 MILES
BUOYS

LACHINE
COURSE
1870

ISLE DORVAL

BUSHY ISLAND

1000  500  0    1000

*The course at Lachine, near Montreal, 1870.*

to the rudder of the *Dunston*, since the eddies and currents on the Lachine course required a larger working rudder surface than was usual on the Tyne.

The railway men were again of service when the press of callers became too much. On the day before the race an American, who said he was from the West, not only overstayed his welcome, but also asked James Taylor how much the English crew would accept to throw the race. He was shown the door and invited to watch the next day to see what the Tynesiders thought of his proposition. A hint that their help would be appreciated and 50 railwaymen arrived early on the morning of the race to guard the perimeter of the cottage and the boathouse. Nobody was allowed to enter without express permission from the crew or their connections.

Forty thousand dollars (£7,460) were gambled on the result of the race, and it would have been more if the Canadians had understood that if the book will not balance, then odds ought to be given. The English contingent scraped together as much money as they could to gamble at evens but they calculated that 10,000 dollars more would have been wagered on the St John crew if they had been able to cover it. As it was, a Mr Joseph Newton, who was carrying sufficient funds to finance a forthcoming trip to California, was persuaded to part with his money so that the Tyneside party

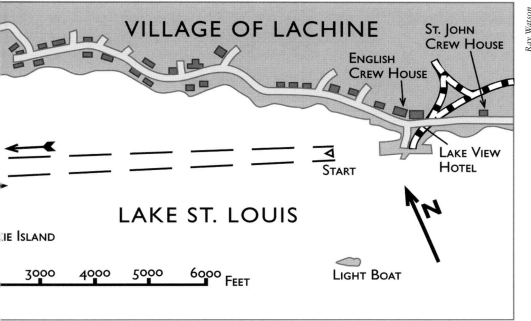

could accommodate eager Canadian backers. In a two horse, or boat, race you only have to stop one party to be sure of the other winning, so it is not surprising that the Tynesiders were anxious about interference.

Twenty thousand people arrived by train from Montreal, a distance of ten miles, and disembarked onto specially constructed timber platforms. Many others came on horseback or in carriages of all descriptions. The scene was set for a titanic intercontinental battle. The St John, New Brunswick crew had won the amateur race at the international regatta in Paris in 1867, and had remained unbeaten in North America ever since. A very different Tyne Champion Four, stroked by the late Bob Chambers, of which James Taylor was the only survivor, had won the professional watermen's race in Paris. Renforth's men were worthy successors to Chambers's Champion Four and, in defeating the Thames Champions, Surbiton, both on the Thames and the Tyne, had earned the right to represent England in the coming contest.

The race was delayed for over two hours because the St John men were reluctant to row in anything but a flat calm. An early wind had disturbed the surface of the lake but it had died away around midday and although the water remained a little disturbed the Tynesiders were eager to start at 3pm as planned. Eventually the New Brunswickers were persuaded to take to the water and the race got under way at about 5.30pm.

This Anglo-Canadian confrontation was not only a clash of continents, it was also a clash of styles. The St John men, sitting tightly on their seats, bent slightly forward, and brought the oar handle back in a level line to the pit of the stomach. They used their arms and shoulders only to give the necessary propelling power and came back no further than an upright position in the seat. They eschewed the use of footstraps, since they did not go far enough back to need them in the recovery. Their oars also had no 'buttons' on them. The Tyne men went forward to their toes at the beginning of the stroke and were thus able to supplement the force from arms, shoulders and chest with power from the thighs. As the stroke unwound, the legs were used, driving off the foot-board and sliding easily on the seat, before using the footstraps to pull forward again to take the next stroke.

The St John men rowed a short, light elastic arm stroke, which was pretty to look at, quickly got way on the boat, and could be used at rates of up to 50 strokes a minute. The Tyne men pulled a long, even swing, which could not be worked at above 40 strokes a minute without risking becoming so ragged that the boat did not run but jerked its way across the water. However if they could hold in the groove at 38 strokes per minute, the boat could be made to run on in steady unceasing motion.

At the start of the race the St John crew showed in front, stroking 48 to the minute, and leading by half a length at 100 yards. The Tynesiders gradually got into their rhythm and once 100 yards had gone the gap got no wider. After 150 yards Renforth had the measure of the Canadians and drove *Dunston* level within another 50 yards. At 300 yards the Tynesiders had a lead of two lengths and Renforth gave the word to take their opponents' water. Once the St John men began to row in Renforth's backwash their rate dropped to 42 strokes a minute. From this point forth the race became a procession. The New Brunswickers were unable to handle the difficult condi-tions on parts of the course, steered a poor course, and were soundly beaten by 200 yards. The Tyne men rowed a steady 38 strokes a minute until the turn at 3 miles, the halfway point, where they were leading so comfortably they dropped the rate to 36. James Taylor steered a superb line, never wandering off the straight, and taking advan-tage of every eddy or favourable current.

The only conclusion that could be drawn was that the St John crew was severely overmatched. Since the St John men were just as fit, and although not heavier, were rather taller than the Tyne men, the victory must also be seen as a triumph for the row-ing style of the Tynesiders. The fast, arm stroke was shown to be no match for the swinging, thigh thrusting, leg-driving, bottom-sliding stroke of the Tynesiders.

At the finish of the race, the St John crew rowed straight back to their quarters

*Tom Winship, 1871. Winship's first visit to Canada in 1870 was as a member of Renforth's crew. On that occasion he was extremely popular with the Canadian ladies!*

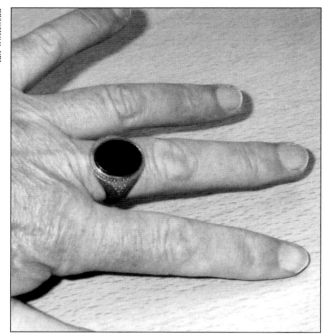

*Inscribed gold signet ring given to Renforth to commemorate the victory at Lachine, 1870*

while Renforth was transferred to the official steamer, *Star*, to make a collection for the losers. The Tyne connections, who had won handsomely, were generous with their donations and $250 was quickly raised for the St John men. Three hours later, while the Tynesiders were celebrating their victory, Renforth suffered a slight fit.

A memento of this victory survives in the form of an inscribed gold signet ring presented to James Renforth. The ring has a large, deep red, stone mounted in it, and the inscription, on the inner surface, reads:

'Presented to James Renforth by his friend John Elliott 15th September 1870 Montreal Tyne Rowing Crew'

John Elliott was Chief Constable of Gateshead and, as becomes clear later, was closely connected with James Renforth. One assumes that he was one of the Tyne Crew's backers on this occasion and had won handsomely on the race. There is no evidence to suggest that Elliott travelled with the crew to Montreal and it is most likely that the ring was given on Renforth's return to England. The ring, which I have seen, is now in private ownership in the North East of England.

The following day, Renforth, Taylor and Winship competed in a sculling race for $150, which Renforth won, seemingly none the worse for his fit the previous day. Winship had been sent a rosette, the previous day, 'put together by fair fingers', together with a request for him to wear it during the skiff race and to raise his hand if he was in the lead when he passed his admirer's house. He clearly remained popular with the Canadian ladies, but beating Renforth was not so easy. Renforth had been unable to persuade any of the American scullers to take him on in a match and there was no reason to delay the return to England. The boats which the Tyne party had brought with them from England were sold.

Walter Brown, the American sculler who had defeated William Sadler on the Tyne in 1869, bought Renforth's skiff *William Blakey*. The other boats were auctioned. The race-winning four, *Dunston* fetched $250 (£50), and the skiff, *Derwenthaugh* $100 (£20). The experimental four *Jarrow*, did not reach its reserve price, with $200 being the highest bid, and it was bought in.

The crew arrived back in Newcastle on Tuesday 4th October 1870 to be greeted by a huge crowd at Newcastle's Central Station. Renforth was lifted shoulder high to a cab in which he was then conveyed to the Adelaide Hotel. He even gave an impromptu performance of a local parody on the song 'Nothing More' and followed that with other comic songs.

At this moment it must have appeared to the outside world that the Canadian adventure had been a huge success, and that the victorious four would now go on from strength to strength. In reality a huge rift had opened up between Renforth and Taylor over the selection of *Dunston*, and not *Jarrow*, to row in the big race. Since so much was at stake, they had hidden their differences until they were back on Tyneside, but bitter conflict was once again about to break out within the Champion Four.

*An advertisement from a trade directory of 1880 demonstrates the popularity of skiff racing.*

# Home and Alone

Even as the celebrations of the victory over the Canadians began to die down, James Renforth must have been wondering if he had made the biggest mistake of his life. The Svengali-like James Taylor was not only a formidable oarsman, he was by the distance from the High Level Bridge to the Skinner Burn the smartest of the professional rowers when it came to the land-based side of the business. He was also widely regarded as the brains behind Renforth's success.

It was he that had trained and guided James to victory over Harry Kelley and he that had brought the young man into the Champion Four. Easily the longest serving member of the Champion crew, Taylor had controlled and connived at the changes in line-up over the last four years and had both stroked the boat and foot-steered it from the bow seat. Now Renforth had fallen out with his mentor: and all over the best design for a racing boat

For the moment Renforth returned to the Sir Charles Napier Inn and picked up business where he had left off. Joseph Sadler had accepted a challenge from the Australian sculler, Michael Rush, but Renforth felt that the challenge should have come

*Newcastle Libraries*

*Newcastle Quayside c.1880. Queen Street is off the Quayside, to the right*

to him as champion. He offered to race against Sadler with the winner to meet Rush. Sadler's response was to write, stressing that he was not claiming to be champion, but asserting his right to row against whom he pleased. However he had no wish to take on Renforth, whom he accepted was the best, but said that he regarded himself as the second best man in England.

At about the same time a challenge was sent to Renforth by Robert Fulton, the stroke of the St John crew. Fulton was, of course, completely unaware of the split in the Tyne Four, but the arrival of his challenge held out the prospect of a lucrative return visit to Canada for whoever could lay claim to being the Tyne champions. As well as the match with the St John crew there was to be a large and richly endowed regatta in Halifax, Nova Scotia which promised to make any transatlantic foray doubly rewarding. When the previous split had occurred between Taylor and Renforth on the one hand, and Scott and Thompson on the other, the affair had been settled with a pair-oar race. A four-oar contest had also been planned, but had fallen through when Scott and Thompson recognised that they were probably heading for another defeat. A pair-oar contest on the Tyne was the most likely route to settle the current dispute.

Renforth was in the worst possible position in that both John Martin and Thomas Winship had sided with James Taylor. Winship and Taylor had won the pair race at the Thames Regatta in 1869 (Renforth had opted for the four and the skiff races) and were regarded as a well-matched and skilful combination. The balance of opinion among the sporting public was that Renforth would struggle without Taylor to guide and support him. If he was to challenge Winship, Martin and Taylor, he would need to find three new men to row in a four with him, and this would be against three-quarters of the battle-hardened Lachine crew. As regards a pair race, there was great speculation as to which of the Tyne oarsmen he would choose to be his partner. Many of the non-partisan supporters of aquatics hoped that the four would sort out their differences. However, when the story of the split started to circulate complete with disparaging additions about him, Renforth decide to act.

On Wednesday 2nd November 1870, a challenge appeared in the *Newcastle Daily Chronicle*:

---

### CHALLENGES.

CHALLENGE TO THE WORLD;—James Renforth, champion sculler, will match two men to row any other two in the world, either as pair-oars or rowing double-sculls, for a stake of £200 a-side. A match can be made either at James Renforth's, the Sir Charles Napier Inn, or at Mr. Jos. Bagnall's Cloth Market, Newcastle, any night between the hours of eight and ten.

---

A meeting was arranged to take place that night in the green room of the Oxford Music Hall. Renforth formally repeated his challenge and William Blakey, acting for Winship and Taylor, accepted the pair-oar option and asked Renforth to name his partner. How clearly Renforth's isolation is shown. He was acting for himself, negotiating with a former supporter of his – if you remember the skiff Renforth sold to Walter Brown in Canada was named *William Blakey* – who was representing his opponents.

Renforth hesitated, and said that he could not name his mate just then as the oarsman he had chosen had not yet given his consent for the match. The champion put down a fiver with the owner of the Oxford, Joshua Bagnall, and asked to be allowed to name his partner at the second deposit, which would be in 16 days time. William Blakey refused to agree to this and for a moment it looked as if the match would fall through. Suddenly, Renforth conceded the point and named the famous Thames rower Henry Kelley as his partner. This was a huge surprise as it had been assumed that Renforth would choose another Tyne man. Nobody had considered that he might go as far afield as the Thames to find a partner. Cocknies were there to be beaten, as in the music hall song *The Defeat of the Cocknies* composed to commemorate the great victories at the Thames Regatta of 1868, not to be welcomed into the boat! But Renforth's actions were not without precedent. Harry and Robert Clasper had combined with the Coombes brothers of London to win the fours at the Thames Regatta of 1849. But that was recruiting Thames men to row on their home river, and would also have saved on expenses, remembering that this was a professional sport.

Harry Kelley was both admired as an oarsman and very well liked on Tyneside. The problem he and Renforth faced was that they had never rowed together; they lived at opposite ends of the country; they both had pubs to run and they had contrasting strokes. Even if Kelley consented to taking part it would be no easy task to get ready by 16th January 1871. And even then, in their first contest together they would have to do battle against the established and accomplished pair Winship and Taylor.

Kelley's response was swift and positive. On Friday 4th November he sent a telegram to Renforth announcing that he was perfectly willing to row, and moreover he would put up £100, ie half of their stake. By the Monday Renforth was on the train to London so that he and Kelley could take a few days practice together on the Thames.

How this practice went was a closely guarded secret, but on his return to Newcastle Renforth remained hopeful that he and Kelley would make a good pair. There were rumours that Renforth would forfeit his first instalment of the stake and no more would be heard of the Tyne-Thames partnership. For the moment Kelley and Renforth had to train separately on Thames and Tyne, but the instalments of the stake continued to go down and the match remained very much on.

On Saturday 3rd December 1870, a letter from James Taylor to the *Newcastle Daily Chronicle* was published.

> **TO THE EDITOR OF THE DAILY CHRONICLE.**
>
> SIR,—I see by your paper of the 1st December that the Tyne crew is invited to take part in the forthcoming regatta at Halifax, Nova Scotia, and as it is intended to enter some other crew, I think it my duty to inform the public that the Tyne crew still exists (at least three of them stick together), and that they intend to take part against all comers at the proposed regatta.—I am, yours respectfully,
>
> JAMES TAYLOR (for Tyne Crew).
>
> Trafalgar Inn, New Bridge Street, Newcastle, Dec. 1870.

Crews were often referred to by the name of their stroke – Clasper's crew, Chambers's crew etc. In the tricky case now unfolding, what was the Tyne crew was also Renforth's crew, but he was no longer with his companions. Challenges and invitations were coming from across the Atlantic for the 'Tyne crew' which had triumphed at Lachine. Should Renforth and any crew he might gather around him be the ones to take up the invitations, or should the other three from the Lachine boat make the journey? Taylor was determined to lay claim to the title, 'Tyne crew', which he hoped would mean that it would be he and his companions who went to Canada in 1871. The pair-oar race was still six weeks away and no mention had yet been made of a contest in fours, but the battle of words had begun.

Kelley finally arrived in Newcastle on Friday 9th December and was met at Central Station by Renforth. They immediately installed themselves at the Dun Cow Inn, Dunston, which they intended to use as their training quarters. Both Renforth and Kelley had used the Dun Cow as a training base previously and they were happy to settle in close to Robert Jewitt's boat-building yard.

The final winding up of business concerning the Lachine match took place at this time. Backers received a dividend of six shillings in the pound – a return of 30 per cent on money which had only been tied up for six months. At a time of low inflation, when dividends were historically small, investing in professional rowing was good business – as long as the crew you had staked won!

Serious training on the river now commenced while the pair waited for Robert Jewitt to complete a new boat, specially designed to accommodate two men of their weight and power.

River watchers were anxious to see how Kelley and Renforth rowed together and a large crowd gathered to observe their first outing. The verdict was not at all flattering. Renforth pulled the traditional Tyne stroke, lying low to his work, sliding on his seat, and rounding his back. Kelley sat high to the oar, was steady on his seat and swung back and forth in an even, mechanical motion. The Londoner's rowlock was also too high, which only added to their difficulties.

Fortunately, after an adjustment to the rowlock and a few more outings, the pair began to row well together. The launch of their new boat, the *Dunston,* added to the growing feeling of confidence. Taylor and Winship also had a new boat, the *Jarrow,* built by James's brother Matt to Armstrong's design. The grudge which had started at Lachine in a dispute over boat design was to be continued thousands of miles to the east on the river Tyne. Would *Dunston* or *Jarrow* prevail?

In the days leading up to Christmas, Renforth was unable to train because of a troublesome boil on his backside. The sliding technique used by Tyneside oarsmen to lengthen their stroke was very tough on the skin and boils were a frequent side effect of the method. The eventual development of a successful sliding seat must have been a great relief, but that was still some months away.

Although the split between professional and amateur oarsmen was continuing to widen, Renforth and Kelley were invited to speak at the Tyne Amateur Rowing Club's Annual Dinner on 23rd December. Kelley attended but it appears that Renforth's condition did not even allow him to sit down comfortably to dinner.

Just as worrying for the heavyweight pairing was the state of the Tyne. Severe wintry weather meant that the championship course was studded with great masses of floating ice and snow. Renforth and Kelley made plans to travel up the coast to Blyth to train if, once Renforth was fit again, the iceberg count on the Tyne was still high.

Renforth and Kelley were able to train on the Tyne for a few days after Christmas, until on New Year's Eve the river froze over completely. The contingency plan to relocate to Blyth fell through because that river was also frozen. Taylor and Winship continued to train on the Tyne, but closer to the sea, working out of the Jarrow boathouse. Renforth and Kelley, who so desperately needed practice in the boat together, had to content themselves with walking exercise of at least ten miles a day. Once the ice had broken up a bit they walked from Dunston each day to Matt Scott's riverside inn near Low Felling to train on the lower reaches of the Tyne. This is perhaps an indication that there were no hard feelings between Renforth and Scott, who had been one of the victims of the previous split of the then Champion Four in 1869. Even now that they were able to get on the river, Renforth and Kelley encountered another problem when they collided with a piece of floating ice. *Dunston* was holed in the stern and filled up with water. Unperturbed, they practised in an old boat that same afternoon while *Dunston* underwent repairs.

The *Chronicle* columnist 'Scotswood' expressed an opinion that the Tyne-Thames pair was ugly to watch but strong. He also had concerns as to whether or not Kelley

*It is hard to believe the Tyne would freeze over in winter, but occasionally it did. This painting dates from the mid-18th century.*

could hold Renforth. Yet another factor he considered was what might happen if the race had to be rowed downriver because of the ice. James Taylor was a wherryman, used to piloting the large wherries (lighters) to load coal onto ships on the lower Tyne. He knew all the currents and eddies in that part of the river which would form the course, if the ice upriver did not disperse. This would give him a big advantage over Kelley, who would foot-steer the opposing pair from the bow, because being a Londoner, Kelley was only familiar with the usual championship course.

Confusion continued as to who might make up any 'Tyne crew' to attend the Halifax Regatta. The *Chronicle* thought it might be any one of three crews and suggested that they ought to race to see who should represent the Tyne. Two days before the big race betting was 7 to 4 on Renforth and Kelley.

Before going on to describe the race it is perhaps worth making a small digression into the two 'schools' of professional rowing on the Tyne. Renforth, after a brief appearance in a Northern Rowing Club four early in his career, had been poached by the Albion Rowing Club and had quickly become the star oarsman of that school. His split with Taylor and the other members of the Lachine crew had necessitated a shift in the direction of the other camp. Hence the sudden appearance of Joshua Bagnall, the president of the Northern Rowing Club and its principal supporter, in connection with the conduct of Renforth's business. The allegiances, and commercial considerations underpinning them, are nicely encapsulated in the chosen locations for the depositing of the stake in this pair-oar match.

| | | | |
|---|---|---|---|
| 1st deposit | £5 | at Joshua Bagnall's Wheatsheaf Inn | Northern |
| 2nd deposit | £20 | at William Blakey's Adelaide Hotel | Albion |
| 3rd deposit | £25 | at James Renforth's Sir Charles Napier Inn | Independent |
| 4th deposit | £25 | at James Taylor's Trafalgar Inn | Albion |
| 5th deposit | £25 | at Joshua Bagnall's Wheatsheaf Inn | Northern |
| 6th deposit | £25 | at James Renforth's Sir Charles Napier Inn | Independent |
| 7th deposit | £75 | at offices of the *Newcastle Chronicle* | final stakeholder |

Deposits 2 to 6 were made on successive Friday nights to maximise trade in the principals' pubs. Renforth was fortunate in that he hosted two Friday night 'plankings', but perhaps that was a perk of being the champion, or possibly because the challenge had originated with him.

At the depositing of the final £75 of the stake, William Oldham was chosen to referee the contest after Renforth had rejected William Blakey's choice of Mr Johns of the Tyne Amateur Rowing Club, or 'any amateur referee' – a sign perhaps of hardening attitudes in the great debate over professionalism in rowing.

The race took place on the morning of Monday 16th January 1871, and despite a squally south-westerly wind and showers of driving rain, a big crowd turned out to watch. As well as occupying the usual vantage points on the bridges, on both banks of the Tyne, and on King's Meadows island, passage aboard steam boats was greatly in demand. Fares ranged from two shillings up to ten shillings for a place on the referee's boat, the *Walker* – half a week's wages for an ordinary working man – but she was soon full, although not with ordinary working men. As was customary, the *Chronicle* published the vital statistics of the combatants.

| | Height | Weight | Age |
|---|---|---|---|
| | ft. in. | st. lbs. | |
| James Renforth | 5 7½ | 11 2 | 28 |
| Henry Kelley | 5 8½ | 11 3 | 39 |
| | Total | 22 5 | 67 |
| | | | |
| Thomas Winship | 5 7½ | 11 0 | 27 |
| James Taylor | 5 7½ | 10 2 | 34 |
| | Total | 21 2 | 61 |

Betting was heavy, with the 7 to 4 on Renforth and Kelley being eagerly taken by Winship and Taylor's supporters. As a result the starting price shifted to 11 to 8 on the Tyne-Thames pairing. Both crews were well-wrapped up against the cold when they took to the water soon after 10am. Taylor and Winship were wearing their blue club caps: Renforth and Kelley, perhaps wishing to demonstrate the eclectic origins of their partnership, wore tartan caps. Renforth was his usual ebullient self, waving his cap gaily above his head in response to the cheering. Kelley sat sedately in the boat, conserving his energies for the race. As was often the case in professional rowing, Renforth and Kelley used their warm-up to display a lack of skill and unanimity in their stroke in the cause of securing a better price for their backers. Only the unwary can have been fooled since they still started as odds-on favourites. Tyne oarsmen customarily rowed stripped to the waist, but all four men retained their flannel body shirts and Kelley kept his cap on too. As the old man of the race, at 39, and rowing bow, he was feeling the effects of the biting wind.

At the start Winship and Taylor were rating 44 strokes per minute to Renforth and Kelley's 40, and were able to hold their heavyweight opponents for a short while. But before 100 yards had been covered Renforth and Kelley began to draw ahead. Winship and Taylor continued to row well together but Renforth and Kelley were powering through the waves, 'as steadily as an ironclad' was how the *Chronicle* put it. Renforth and Kelley were already a length clear at the Skinner Burn and shot over to take their opponents' water, and to give them their backwash. Once they had straightened up they were only half a length clear, and Winship and Taylor made a huge effort, encouraged by the knowledge that if they could close this gap Renforth and Kelley would have to return to their own side or risk a foul.

A sudden squall broke on both crews, raising even more of a swell and making rowing extremely difficult. Renforth gave the word for an extra pull and, lying to their work with tremendous energy the heavyweights drew away from the Tyne pair. At the brand new Redheugh Bridge they led by three lengths. Renforth and Kelley were now progressing steadily at 39 strokes a minute while Winship and Taylor were already showing signs of distress. As a contest the race seemed to be over.

After passing the Leadworks Shot Tower the leaders veered off the usual course, moving southwards towards the middle of the river. The reason for this detour soon became clear to the passengers aboard the following steamers. The shortest route to the channel between the Annie Islet and the Haughs was a mass of jagged, floating ice. Renforth and Kelley headed for what seemed the most open section of the ice field, but before they reached it, the stem of their boat caught against a submerged floe. Luckily they had just eased to half-speed, and *Dunston*, instead of being cut open, was only

*Redheugh Bridge c.1889. Nearing completion in January 1871, the drifting ice that had troubled Renforth and Kelley carried all its scaffolding down river and out to sea.*

turned to one side. Renforth and Kelley were now at a dead stand-still, and a great shout went up from the spectators, who thought for a moment that the boat was holed. Winship and Taylor, who were directly behind, rowed right up to them, but then stopped to avoid a foul. Both pairs now searched for an opening in the ice and got through quite close to one another.

Renforth and Kelley rowed hard to the north, intent on reverting to the usual course inside the Annie. A man standing on the end of the islet warned them of ice in the channel and they were forced to head south once more. This extraordinary turn of events presented a golden opportunity to Winship and Taylor, who had remained in mid-river, but Taylor was dead beat and Winship could not apply the power for fear of driving them off course. Both pairs passed between the Annie and the (King's) Meadows island with Renforth and Kelley going back into the lead. Renforth's efforts to put the race beyond doubt began to overpower his companion and several times the *Dunston* was nearly driven ashore on the Meadows. The unsteady course followed by

*Elswick Leadworks Shot Tower, a Tyne landmark, 1900.*

the Tyne-Thames pair gave encouragement to the supporters of Winship and Taylor and cries of 'Had away the lightweights' rang out. At the Meadows public house, after about 1½ miles, the heavyweights had a lead of eight or nine lengths and it was clear that Winship and Taylor could not respond to their followers' urgings. Renforth and Kelley now took things easy and as they approached the finish Renforth waved his hand above his head in his characteristic acknowledgement of the plaudits which greeted the pair. They finished with a tremendous spurt, passing under the Scotswood Suspension Bridge the winners by 200 yards. Renforth and Kelley were taken aboard the referee's boat where they made the usual collection for their beaten opponents, £13 8s being raised.

It was an astounding victory. Renforth and Kelley had got away from their opponents once, and then when the ice blocked their path, they had zigzagged their way upriver. They had rowed much further than Winship and Taylor but had still won as they pleased by 200 yards. Jewitt had built a boat completely out of copper over the preceding weekend for them to negotiate ice safely but they had decided not to use it: a decision that they must have regretted as they crashed into the submerged floe and viewed the prospect of making their way through more of the same.

The *Chronicle* gave a full analysis of the heavyweights' triumph and its probable effect on the professional rowing scene. It was now considered highly unlikely that the Lachine four would re-form. But it was expected that the St John crew would consent to row against a new four recruited by Renforth. The *Chronicle*'s remarks about Renforth provide a contemporary view of his achievement in stroking *Dunston* to victory.

> **To Renforth the victory must have been particularly gratifying. Acknowledged to be invincible everywhere else, the increasing depreciation he had to undergo from certain parties at home had caused many to forget the great feats by which he first made himself a name. By his wonderful exhibition of oarsmanship yesterday he has rubbed up the memories of the opposition most effectually, and we shall probably hear no more of the scullers challenges with which he was threatened. It is indubitable that the champion's wonderful physique is not in the smallest degree impaired, and that his skill with the oar is greater than ever. Renforth has indeed attained a proud position amongst oarsmen – such a position as was never previously attained by any victor of the oar, and apparently he is but at the commencement of his career, having been little more than four years before the public.**

*Newcastle Daily Chronicle* Tuesday 17th January 1871

Renforth's period of professional isolation was drawing to a close. Just four months after the initial split with James Taylor he was in a position to build a new four around himself in preparation for another Canadian campaign.

# Going West – Again

The day after their victory, Renforth and Kelley attended a benefit performance of the pantomime *Robin Hood* at the Tyne Theatre. At the end of the show the pair appeared on stage and Kelley said a few words in appreciation of the reception they had received. There were calls for Renforth to speak and although it was well known that he disliked public speaking, for a moment it appeared that he might address the audience. The thunder of applause as he stepped forward completely disconcerted him and he was reduced to bowing his acknowledgement of the noisy reception. He must have felt that his position as the popular hero of Tyneside was once again secure and that he could concentrate on gathering a crew to take on the St John men on their home water.

The formal position on the transatlantic challenge was resolved within four days of Renforth and Kelley's victory. Articles were sent to Canada offering a contest with only one man on each side being named. It was hoped that the match would be able to proceed on the basis that it would be rowed between Robert Fulton and three Canadians, and Renforth and three English oarsmen. This would enable business matters to take their course without Renforth being under unreasonable pressure to name his crew. Speculation on the make up of the crew was rife. Renforth appeared at Manley's Circus at Gateshead in the company of James Percy, John Bright and Henry Kelley, but nothing was revealed as to whom Renforth would choose.

Renforth's confidence was high. He knew he was the best sculler, and probably the best stroke, in the world; he had forged a partnership with the man considered by many to be the next best oarsman currently in training; and he would have his pick of a group of highly competent Tyne oarsmen to complete his four. A challenge (see page 110) appeared in the *Newcastle Daily Chronicle* of Monday 6th February 1871.

Fame was not sufficient to guarantee fortune and drinkers still needed to be attracted to the pub, so Renforth took the usual steps to bring them in. He continued to coach other rowers, which meant that some of the deposits for races were made at the Sir Charles Napier. This brought him into direct opposition with James Taylor, who was frequently engaged in coaching the opponents of Renforth's charges. Several times they made their way up river on the same official steamer, with Renforth coaching from the bow and Taylor from the paddle box. Renforth also organised an open-

" James Renforth, Champion of England, will match his four-oared crew to row any four in the world the following races, viz., a four-oared race, a pair-oared race, and a sculler's race, for from £200 to £500 a-side, the race or races to take place eight weeks after the first deposit is made. The four-oared race may be rowed with or without coxswains, as may be agreed upon at the time of making the match. Answers addressed to James Renforth, at his house, the Sir Charles Napier Inn, Queen Street, Newcastle ; Mr. J. H. Baird, Star Inn, Northumberland Street, Newcastle ; or the Editor of the 'Newcastle Daily Chronicle,' will receive immediate attention."

*The challenge that appeared in the Newcastle Daily Chronicle on 6th May.*

boat handicap on the Tyne on Good Friday and Easter Saturday, offering as a first prize his own splendid new open-boat *Ethel*, and a gold ring as second prize. All entries to be made only to James Renforth at the Sir Charles Napier Inn.

At the end of March news came through from Canada that Renforth's articles, in which the 'Tyne' crew would be made up of Renforth and three other English oarsmen, were acceptable to the St John men. The *Chronicle* appealed for public support, pointing out that this £1,000 race on the other side of the Atlantic was a big undertaking for Renforth. It does appear that, having split from Taylor, Renforth had assumed something of his former mentor's role. He was the one making the decisions, choosing the crew, and taking responsibility for the business side of the challenge. A meeting of backers and supporters was called for Tuesday 14th April 1871, to be held at the Sir Charles Napier Inn, in order to discuss the question of raising the cash for the £500 stake and the expenses. £200 expenses was being contributed by supporters of the St John crew, in recognition of the costs that would be incurred in bringing the English crew across the Atlantic, but the balance would need to be made up by local supporters. At the same time Renforth took the opportunity of making it clear that Henry Kelley had agreed to be in the crew. The prospect of the champion and ex-champion making up half of the four should encourage putative backers to be bold with their money.

Fifteen minutes after the start of the meeting, the cash for stake and expenses had been pledged and discussion was able to turn to the conduct of the campaign. It was thought that Robert Jewitt should be asked to build a new boat for the race. As regards the make up of the crew it was agreed that Renforth would try several oarsmen and select the best men from among the triallists.

Having confirmed arrangements for the trip to North America, Renforth once again tried to drum up rowing business, and by association, pub trade, by offering fours, pairs, or skiff races for £200 a-side on the Monday preceding Newcastle Races. Kelley arrived in the North East on Wednesday April 26th, to be met by his long time backer and friend, J. H. Baird of the Star Hotel, together with James Renforth and James Percy. Kelley and Renforth attended Morpeth races on the Thursday, but on Friday the first trial of the four would take place.

*James Percy*

The initial crew was John Bright (bow), Robert Chambers, Henry Kelley, James Renforth (stroke). While out on the river they pulled up at Robert Jewitt's Dunston boathouse so he could size them up in preparation for building the boat they would take with them to America. It was thought that these four would make up the crew, with James Percy being taken as the spare man. At Lachine, one of the crew's backers, John Adams, had acted as spare man, but he had been nowhere near fit or skilled enough to hold his own in the boat. In the light of that experience it made sense to take Percy, who was a thoroughly competent oarsman. After a few days of rowing as part of this four, Kelley returned to London and training for the great international contest ceased for the moment.

Training was due to recommence around the 16th May, but Kelley was unavoidably delayed in London, so James Percy took his place in the boat. The campaign almost struck disaster within a few days. Renforth had determined to put in an appearance on the river in honour of 'barge day', which this year fell on 18th May. 'Barge day' was a traditional day for rowing races to be held on the Tyne; one of the first regattas having taken place on Ascension Day 1830, to accompany the ceremonial beating of the bounds of the River Tyne by the mayoral barge. Percy, Chambers, Bright and Renforth, together with a coxswain, were out in the Northern Club's boat *Robert Jewitt* when Robert Chambers broke his oar. The boat swung round broadside and was rowed down by a foyboat coming down river. The crew were all thrown in the water. Renforth took care of the coxswain, and with Percy, who was also an excellent swimmer, swam to some steamboats lying nearby. Both Chambers and Bright were non-swimmers but they were quickly pulled from the water and put on board a steamer. None was any the worse for the experience although Percy, in trying to swim ashore from one of the steamboats, was drawn under the craft's bottom and narrowly escaped drowning.

Kelley arrived back in Newcastle on 22nd May, but Renforth's crew did not begin hard training until the 7th June. The plan was to leave for New Brunswick about the second week in July. It was hoped that they might be able to use *Dunston-on-Tyne*, which had been sold in Canada for $250 after the Lachine race, as spare boat. Jewitt was to build a new boat, and if the use of *Dunston* could not be secured, he would build two.

On the 1st June 1871 a mischievous challenge from the up and coming sculler Robert Bagnall appeared in the *Newcastle Daily Chronicle*. Bagnall was coached by James Taylor, the master of the needling challenge, and this example was well up to his coach's standard.

> ROBERT BAGNALL, of the Ouseburn, Newcastle, will take 200 yards start and row James Renforth a match on the Tyne in skiffs, from the High Level Bridge to Scotswood Suspension Bridge, according to the champion's own offer, for any sum he chooses to name. An early answer through the "Chronicle" will meet with attention.

Renforth made an imperious reply, pointing out that the 200 yards he had offered was at the finish of a six mile race, not, as Bagnall had wilfully misrepresented it, at the start of a less than four mile contest.

The professional vs amateur argument rumbled on. Increasingly, Aquatics reports in the *Chronicle* included accounts of minor races between amateurs. The separation of amateur and professional rowing meant that many amateurs were no longer interested in professional racing, which was bound to be to the detriment of the professionals. The amateur clubs had wanted to stage an amateurs-only regatta on the Tyne, to which the professional clubs, the Albion and the Northern, had responded by organising a professional regatta to take place on the 15th and 16th June. As with the Thames Regatta, competitors were only allowed to enter for two races. Renforth opted for the fours and the pairs, with Kelley. Kelley had been suffering from sciatica, but against medical, and Renforth's, advice, decided to row in the pair race. In poor weather Renforth and Kelley were soundly beaten by Taylor and Winship. Poor Kelley was too ill to make any substantial contribution to the pairing and Renforth frequently rowed with one hand to avoid turning the boat.

The following day Renforth had the satisfaction of stroking his four to victory over Winship's crew, which included James Taylor. Percy, rowing bow, stood in for the indisposed Kelley, while Chambers sat at 2 and Bright at 3. At the finish both Renforth and

112

*The Winship Four of 1871. From left, Tom Winship, Robert Bagnall, Joseph Sadler, James Taylor. This was the crew that made first, and winning, use of the American pattern of sliding seat on the Tyne in 1871.*

Bright were rowing with one hand, but this time it was so they could wave to the crowd with the other. On Monday 19th June, James Taylor issued a challenge in the *Newcastle Daily Chronicle* (see following page) – a stark example of how much Renforth was feared as an opponent by those who knew the true extent of his skill and strength with the oar. The only participation allowed for Renforth was in one of four sculling matches. Kelley was unfit, and in any case Robert Bagnall was the coming man. Taylor would have been confident that Bagnall would beat everybody but Renforth, so Taylor would win £300 and lose £100 – good business by any standard.

At some point, before he went into serious training, Renforth sold the Sir Charles Napier Inn to a Mr Fisher and settled into a house in James Street, Gateshead. It was a sensible move to make because, with another transatlantic adventure coming up, the champion would not be able to put the required time and effort into running the pub.

The new four, *England*, built by Robert Jewitt for Renforth's crew, was launched on Monday June 19th. At the same time there was a threat to drop the Patrons Plate, the professional four oared race from the Durham Regatta, supposedly because of a shortage of money. The decision was reconsidered and the race returned to the programme. Renforth's and Winship's crews both promised to compete this year.

Taylor was doing great things as coach of the Tynemouth Amateur Rowing Club. He went with them to the Henley Regatta, but had to return to look after his marquee on Newcastle's Town Moor during Race Week. Even without his presence, Fawcus of Tynemouth won the Diamond Sculls, beating Goldie of Cambridge in what was the first appearance at Henley of a representative of the Tyne amateurs.

Kelley went south again to try and get over his bout of sciatica while the rest of Renforth's crew settled into their training quarters at the Borough Arms, Borough Road, Gateshead – a pub that still stands today. Twice a day they walked down to Robert Jewitt's Dunston boathouse where *England* was kept. Each outing was usually over 5 miles or so, rowed at good speed. Kelley returned at the end of June, replacing John Bright in the number 3 seat, and performing with great style. As long as he was fit the Londoner was an automatic choice, and Bright probably suffered in the trials by being in and out of the 3 spot instead of competing directly with Percy for the bow seat. Robert Chambers, who for a short while in 1868 had been a member of the Champion Four, had made the number 2 seat his own, while Percy was proving a reliable bow man and consummate exponent of foot steering.

On Tuesday July 4th Renforth's crew duly won the Patrons Plate very easily. The *Chronicle* had been saying for days that the Durham race would be too dull to attract

*David Clasper*

*Renforth's crew of 1871, which took part in the tragic race at St John, New Brunswick, Canada. Clockwise from left, James Percy, Robert Chambers, Harry Kelley, James Renforth and John Bright (spare man).*

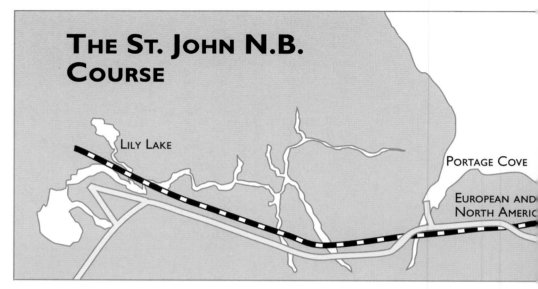

# THE ST. JOHN N.B. COURSE

LILY LAKE

PORTAGE COVE

EUROPEAN AND
NORTH AMERIC

*The St John, New Brunswick, Canada, course, 1871.*

Renforth and his men. Winship's crew had travelled to Bristol to take part in the Regatta there. Once again Renforth showed his feeling for the history of the sport by turning out at the traditional regatta in Durham.

The day after this victory, an afternoon meeting was held of backers of the English crew at Mr Baird's Star Hotel, Northumberland Street, Newcastle. The remaining half of the stakes for the Canadian match was gathered in together with seven shillings in the pound for expenses. Renforth then suggested that the crew should row an official trial for the satisfaction of the men who had put up the money. The chairman of proceedings asked Renforth if he was satisfied with his crew and his boat and the champion said he was. That evening a six mile out and back trial was rowed to the delight of all present. Jewitt had been asked to build another boat on the same lines as the *England* and it was expected to be ready for when the crew left Newcastle in a week's time.

Training tapered off during the last week before taking passage to Canada. The only time the crew expected to go out on the river was when they tried out their new boat, which Robert Jewitt had nearly finished.

A crowd of 3,000 turned out on the afternoon of Wednesday 12th July to see the crew off from the Newcastle Central Station. Even the members of the opposing school, James Taylor and John Martin of the Lachine crew, and the owner of the

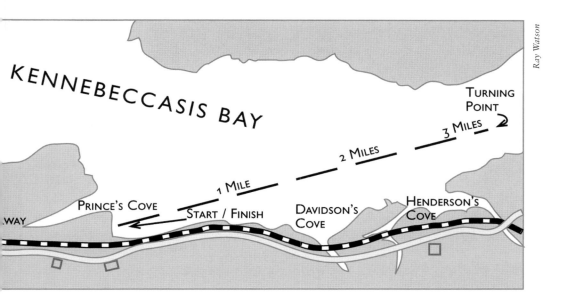

KENNEBECCASIS BAY

TURNING
POINT
3 MILES ⌐

2 MILES

1 MILE

PRINCE'S COVE

START / FINISH

DAVIDSON'S
COVE

HENDERSON'S
COVE

.WAY

*Ray Watson*

Adelaide Hotel, William Blakey, were on hand to wish them good luck. A special carriage had been reserved to take Renforth and his men, the two fours, *England* and *Queen Victoria*, and Renforth's new skiff, to Liverpool. All the boats were in wooden cases secured on top of the roof of the carriage, and there was a short delay when it was realised that one of the fours was sitting above a row of lighted lamps let into the roof of the carriage. Before the train left the lamps were removed to ensure that there was no fire. Amid scenes of great enthusiasm, the train moved out of the station. After arrival in Liverpool that night, the crew were due to embark on the Allen liner, *North America* on Friday, for their voyage to Halifax.

Although the crew encountered some rough weather during the crossing, the biggest mishap of the journey was discovered after they had travelled on by train from Halifax to St John. The outriggers for the boats had been left in Halifax, but they were immediately dispatched and caught up with their owners 24 hours later.

The English four arrived in St John on 28th July 1871 and a few days afterwards took up their quarters at Mr. John McGowan's Claremont House, Torryburn, beside the Kennebeccasis river.

For the first week after their arrival the weather hampered their efforts to get back into hard training. Thick fogs, strong winds and heavy rains alternating so the men always returned to the house drenched. It was impossible to get training clothes dry

*Renforth's 1871 crew practising on the Kennebeccasis River. left to right, Percy (bow), Chambers, Kelley, Renforth (stroke).*

and each man had two or three flannel suits hanging dripping on the line. Fortunately, conditions improved the week afterwards, although every man except Kelley suffered some mild ailment or other during the build-up.

The *England* was used exclusively as a practice boat, but about a week before the race *Queen Victoria* was brought out of her case.

Her dimensions were as follows:

| | |
|---|---|
| Length | 41 feet 8 inches |
| Extreme breadth | 18$^{1/2}$ inches |
| Height amidships | 7$^{3/4}$ inches |
| Height forward | 6 inches |
| Height aft | 4 inches |

Her shell was made of Spanish cedar and her frames were of white wood. Her fitted out weight was 94 pounds. The total weight of the Canadians was just one pound more than that of the English although the rangy St John fishermen were considerably taller than their opponents.

The race was to be rowed under Thames Regatta rules, and, since river conditions were best in the early morning, both crews were instructed to be in their boats by 7am.

All the preliminaries had been satisfactorily concluded by the evening of Tuesday 22nd August, the day before the race, and supporters of both crews gathered in St John that night.

Betting was brisk. As well as there being a number of North American gentlemen present who were willing to back the English, William Blakey and other backers from the 'Adelaide' school had recently arrived in St John. They had crossed the Atlantic with Winship's crew who were now in Halifax preparing for the great Regatta which was to take place later in the summer. Blakey and his friends had come on to St John to see their former protégé and his crew race for the honour of the old country, and were active in laying odds on the Englishmen. Two to one on Renforth's crew was being offered and accepted all over the city. At the end of the night it was estimated that something like $150, 000 had been wagered.

The city was full and many visitors preferred to spend the early hours in the street rather than return to crowded lodgings for such a short time. To be sure of catching the race it would be necessary to leave the city by 4am. Even at that early hour the road from St John to Torryburn was crowded with vehicles and pedestrians. Thousands of local supporters walked the whole seven miles, with many sporting the pink ribbon which proclaimed their allegiance to the St John crew. Those wearing the blue and white colours of England came in for a good deal of good natured chaff as their carriages picked their way through the crowd.

By 5am the crew were finishing their breakfast of steaks, chops, potatoes, tea, coffee and milk, and soon afterwards Renforth, Kelley, Percy, Chambers and the *Chronicle* reporter, Joseph Walton, gathered in the room that Renforth and Kelley were sharing. Letters and a bundle of *Chronicle*s had arrived from home and Kelley read out the newspaper report of their voyage across the Atlantic. Renforth sat close by his friend and kept up a lively running commentary on the narrative.

Percy and Chambers returned to their own room to get changed into their rowing clothes while Renforth went out into the garden with Walton. A crowd of 2,000 to 3,000 had gathered, including a rowdy element which made Walton concerned for Renforth's safety. Brushing aside Walton's fears Renforth happily mixed with the crowd, although he was always attended by a small group of supporters. After enjoying his early morning encounter with the crowd, Renforth returned to the house to ready himself for the race.

In bright sunshine and under an almost cloudless sky the Kennebeccasis lay with a still, glassy surface. Scores of large sailing craft used for transporting lumber, so-called 'wood' boats, and two storied river steamers were moored along the course to give spectators good vantage points from which to view the race. Bands of musicians sta-

119

tioned on the decks of the steamers combined inadvertently to provide a cacophony of different tunes. On shore, long trains of open cars were being delivered to the site by shrieking locomotives of the European and North American Railway. In all 9,000 spectators were transported to the course by railway. All the roads were blocked with carriages and it was estimated that 20,000 spectators were present.

William Oldham and John Bright, who had been keeping watch over the English boats through the night, now separated with Oldham going on board the official steamer to assume his role as the English umpire. Bright launched the *Queen Victoria* and awaited the arrival of the crew. A few minutes after 7am a message came that Fulton and his crew, with their boat, were already aboard the official steamer. The English crew took their places in the *Victoria*, Renforth being the first seated. Renforth wore a flannel suit and a brown silk American driving cap. Kelley, Chambers and Percy also wore their flannels, but they opted for their blue club caps. For a while there was no sign of the New Brunswickers, but when Renforth spotted them on the deck of the referee's steamer he called out, 'Gentlemen, are you ready'. The Canadians called back that they were, and their boat, *St John*, was put into the water. The St John men were resplendent in pink shirts and caps.

The toss for stations now took place with St John winning the toss and choosing the western or outside station. The Englishmen were pleased, since, if the spin of the coin had favoured them, they would have chosen the station they had been given. Renforth and his crew stripped off, ready to row, exciting admiration with their hard-muscled torsos.

For a moment it looked as if there would be a delay because no stake boats had been placed at the start. Renforth and Fulton had shown the greatest good manners and common sense from their first encounter at Lachine and they quickly resolved the problem. They agreed to back on to the mooring buoys and start without the use of stake boats. Both boats were soon ready and the word 'Go' was given. The boats moved slowly and smoothly from the mark. The St John crew perhaps got an advantage at the first stroke, with their quick entry, but their bow could not have shown more than 6 inches in the lead. At the second or third stroke *Victoria* was level with the Canadian boat, and before 100 yards had been covered the Englishmen began to draw away. It looked as if Renforth and his men had another famous victory within their grasp. Betting was continuing but the odds had shortened further on the English crew, with bets being taken at 9 to 4 on. They were such an experienced and strong crew that it seemed impossible for the New Brunswickers to row through them once Renforth had control of the race.

# 'Harry, Harry, I have had something.'

At 200 yards the Englishmen were going well within themselves and were in the lead by half a length. Kelley was feeling so confident that he said to Renforth, 'It's all over', meaning that the race was in their grasp. After a quarter mile or so the Londoner noticed that the St John crew was gradually gaining on them so he called out to Renforth, 'Give us a dozen, Jim', – a spurt of 12 strokes. Today's decimal-educated oarsmen usually call for 'ten', but the principle remains the same.

It was at about this point, (different crew members and observers report essentially the same events but sometimes at slightly varying distances into the race) that the bow man, Percy, found that the boat was running inshore. He had to put the rudder hard against Kelley and himself to try and straighten the boat's course. He had heard Kelley ask for the dozen and both men realised that no 'dozen' came from their stroke oar. In the bow Percy was better able to see what was happening and he observed that Renforth was not getting any way on his oar at all. The boat continued to run inshore at Appleby's Wharf. Spectators noticed that Renforth was rocking from side to side. The champion turned his head over his shoulder and said to Kelley, 'Harry, Harry, I have had something'. Kelley replied, 'What is the matter?' and Renforth fell forward, with his right hand coming off his oar. Alarmed, Kelley spoke again, 'Sit up!' he said, and Renforth tried, but immediately fell back into Kelley's lap. His old rival and now trusted friend realised that the race was over, and, holding James in the boat with one hand and grasping his and Renforth's oar with the other, he ordered Percy and Chambers to row ashore as quickly as they could.

The crowd on shore were at first convinced that they were witnessing a 'fixed' race, and yelled and hissed their disapproval. When the boat approached the shore their mood changed when they saw Renforth lying rigid and white in the bottom of the boat. As the boat grounded, Percy jumped out into the water and, with the aid of some men in the crowd, carried Renforth across the railway line and into a cab standing on the road beyond. The St John crew continued with the race, but by now it had become a tragic training exercise, although it should not be forgotten that this was a race with thousands of pounds hanging on the result and they needed to complete the course to ensure that the stakes and side bets could be paid out.

Percy got into the cab with Renforth, who was rubbing his side and they made their way back along the road to the English crew's headquarters at Claremont House. Renforth was agitated at the disaster that had overtaken the English boat and said to Percy, 'Oh, Jim, this is a bad job'. He was clearly in pain and several times asked Percy not to touch him. When they reached Claremont House Percy got him to his bed and, on Renforth's request, took off his shoes and stockings and brought him a drink of water. Percy waited with him until Kelley and Chambers arrived, about 20 minutes after Renforth had been taken out of the boat, and then went to his own room to change out of his wet things.

Soon afterwards Joseph Walton came into the room and asked Renforth what was the matter, and had he had a fit? Renforth replied, 'No, it is not a fit. I will tell you all after. What will they say at home?' Renforth's seeming irritation with the suggestion that he had suffered a fit led Walton to believe that the champion thought he had been sabotaged. Further questioning about what Renforth might have eaten since breakfast received only the repeated reply, 'I'll tell you all about it after.' Walton was obviously already concerned that the champion might have been poisoned. Renforth's remark, 'What will they say at home?' made at about this time, shows that even as he was dying he was worrying about letting down the Tyneside public. The stricken oarsman was becoming delirious and it became pointless to press him further.

Doctors had been called and, arriving after a further half hour, they tried to induce circulation by heating and rubbing Renforth's limbs, but without success. They also attempted to stimulate him with brandy and water but he was thrashing around and resistant to taking brandy. Attempts to bleed him via veins in both arms produced just a few drops of thick black blood from his left arm and nothing from the right. Renforth was sinking rapidly and he cried out indistinctly a few times, 'Oh my poor wife,' which only Walton seems to have heard; 'Oh Harry', the name of the London oarsman who was with him there in the room; and finally, 'Oh Annie', the name of his eight year old daughter. Renforth died at 8.45am. Kelley, who was holding Renforth's head at the moment of his death, wept bitterly as he saw life ebbing away from his friend.

The news spread quickly through the city of St John and all rejoicing at the victory of the local crew ceased. What had been a half-day holiday, called so that citizens could watch the great race, became a full day's closure of all businesses as a mark of respect to the fallen champion. A post mortem was carried out that afternoon, with the cause of death being given as 'congestion of the lungs'. Dr Maclaren, who had attended Renforth when he was taken ill, carried out the post mortem with a Dr Wade of the 78th Highlanders. At the request of Joseph Walton he removed and kept the heart and the stomach and its contents. The local coroner formally opened an inquest and

*Renforth posing in his flannel suit and rowing colours for a studio portrait, 1871.*

adjourned it until the following day, Thursday, 24th August . The deeply shocked members of the English party in Canada, and the thousands of aquatics supporters back in England now tried to make sense of the death of their champion.

In the days immediately after the death of Renforth, the party in Canada found themselves facing financial and moral dilemmas. Firstly, the defeat had left them short of money. They had plunged into the market confidently, offering 2 to 1 on their men, and they had lost all. The only hope they had of recouping their losses was for the crew, with John Bright, the spare man, at number 2, and Robert Chambers moving to stroke, to compete and win at the Halifax Regatta. They promised to give the prize money to Renforth's widow and orphan, but would also have been hopeful of making some money in side bets. Therefore it was important that the inquest be completed as swiftly as possible so they could get back into training. Sitting in a coroner's court giving evidence was poor preparation for a rowing regatta. Secondly, they wanted to do their duty by their friend and return his body to Tyneside in a dignified and fitting manner. The sooner the body was released the sooner it could be dispatched to England with suitable companions to watch over it during the passage.

The inquest reconvened the day after the race. The crux of the matter was simple. Had Renforth died of natural causes, or had he been poisoned? Joseph Walton, Harry Kelley, Robert Liddell, (who had accompanied Renforth on his walkabout before the race) and James Percy were called to give evidence. After considering the manner and the content of his remarks to Kelley and to Joseph Walton they had been suspicious that Renforth had been poisoned. Walton, Kelley and Percy had known Renforth for years and they believed that Renforth thought he had been tampered with, but all his remarks were made while he was dying and they felt that the belief of a distressed and mortally ill man fell far short of being proof. Only 24 hours after the tragedy they all thought that Renforth had died of natural causes. The difficulty that his friends, the coroner, and the world in general, faced was that the mechanism of death remained unexplained, which left scope for rumours and suspicions that he had been murdered using an undetectable poison.

Before discussing the options of poisoning and natural causes I would like briefly to consider a third possibility: that Renforth died from overstraining himself after taking a large dose of a performance enhancing drug. Since there is not a shred of evidence to support this theory, and it was not thought of at all at the time of Renforth's death, it would not normally rate a mention. However there is a persistent rumour in the North-East of England that drug abuse, perhaps of laudanum (tincture of opium), was what killed Renforth. When I started on this project I had expected at least to find some evidence of drug taking in Tyneside professional rowing circles, if not specifically by Renforth himself, to explain the existence of the drug abuse version of the tale, but I could find none. The source of the rumour may well be a slightly ambiguous account of Renforth's death in McCord and Thompson's book, *The Northern Counties from AD 1000*, (Longman, London, 1998). The authors attribute the death to an overdose of 'Yankee dope' – quoting the *Newcastle Chronicle*. A modern interpretation of an 'overdose of Yankee dope' might well be that the oarsman had taken too much of a performance enhancing drug, and his body had been unable to cope with the effects of the drug whilst under the pressure of stroking the boat in a closely contested race. One thinks of the case of the British cyclist Tommy Simpson, who had taken amphetamines to help his performance, but sadly died while climbing Mont Ventoux in the 1967 Tour de France. A reading of the contemporary accounts indicates that this was not considered as a possible cause at the time. The overdose theory was advanced by those who felt that backers of the St John men had intended to administer a sufficient quantity of dope to disable the champion and hamper the performance of the English boat. This could have appeared nothing more than the onset of a sudden illness, with interference being hard to prove. Therefore an amount of poison which went further, and proved fatal to Renforth was certainly an overdose in the eyes of those who adhered to this theory. The proper interpretation of 'an overdose of Yankee dope' therefore becomes a partial poisoning which went wrong. The theory of the performance enhancing drug is certainly a modern red herring. However, if we look at the two causes which were considered at the inquest, and then add to the contemporary evidence the results of some recent medical studies, I believe it is possible to achieve a more satisfactory understanding of Renforth's death than was possible at the time.

Even as Renforth threw up his right arm, dropped his oar and fell half-way forward on his face, before rising again and falling backwards into Kelley's arms, the crowd on shore had yelled and hissed, believing that the race had been 'sold'. The words that Renforth spoke to Kelley as he collapsed in the boat, 'Harry, Harry, I have had something' and his later remark, that it was not a fit and that he would tell all about it directly, led Harry Kelley and Joseph Walton to conclude that Renforth thought he had been sabotaged.

It was not surprising that Renforth might think that he had been poisoned. Even before he had arrived in Canada for the Lachine race in 1870, the American sculler Walter Brown had warned him to watch out for dirty tricks. Renforth had requested the services of an English cook, but you may recall that she had turned out to prefer the inside of the spirit decanter to that of her kitchen, and she had been sacked. A climate of suspicion with regard to food tampering was thus well-established among the England party. Already suspicious, and with the dying words of Renforth further fuelling their concern, Kelley and Walton had asked for a post mortem to be carried out. The difficulty with the poisoning of food theory, which Walton had recognised when he asked Renforth if he had eaten anything since breakfast, was that Renforth had eaten the same food from the same dishes as all the rest of the crew and their supporters, none of whom had shown any signs of ill-health.

At the inquest, when the post mortem had revealed nothing untoward about Renforth's stomach or its contents, Joseph Walton, Harry Kelley and James Percy all declared themselves satisfied that Renforth had died of natural causes. Walton and Kelley had both been suspicious before the post mortem, but Percy, in giving his evidence, said that he had always thought that, although Renforth's symptoms were unlike any other of Renforth's fits, he had not been poisoned. The Hon. Mr Hazen (Judge of the Admiralty Court for New Brunswick) was not convinced by the opinions of the English contingent and still felt that the unusual and sudden death of Renforth was most likely to have been caused by poisoning. Theories of deadly vegetable poisons smeared on Renforth's oar handle and absorbed through the skin gained currency when it became clear that his death was not as the result of something he had eaten.

Joseph Walton had estimated that the night before the race $150,000 (£28,000) had been wagered on the result of the race. There is no particular reason why this betting should arouse suspicion. The backers of the Tynesiders were supremely confident and by offering 2 to 1 on their crew they found plenty of takers among the supporters of the St John crew who, it had been reported, had rowed an extraordinary trial on the previous day. At Lachine the English crew's supporters had found themselves short of funds, which had left some of the Canadian crew's backers unable to find anyone to take their money. This time William Blakey and his friends had ensured that they had access to plenty of money to accommodate the supporters of the St John crew and that was, at least in part, the reason that the gambling was so heavy on the race.

There was further heavy betting at the start, which Joseph Walton found suspicious, and after the English boat showed in the lead off the start, 9 to 4 was laid several times. This was perfectly normal however: reports of many of the races on the Tyne show gambling continuing right through a contest with greatly fluctuating odds depending on who held the lead. The motive for poisoning is very clear: backers of the St John crew stood to gain enormously from Renforth's collapse. William Blakey and William Oldham, who were two of the heaviest losers on the race, remained convinced that Renforth had been poisoned. However despite the strong motive for poisoning, the shared dishes and good health of the rest of the party, and the normal appearance of the stomach and its contents at the post mortem, weigh heavily against poisoning being the cause of Renforth's death.

Since it was well known that Renforth suffered from epilepsy the first thought of many was that he had experienced some sort of fit which had led to his death. The *Newcastle Daily Journal* had at first reported his collapse as a fit, and it was an obvious conclusion to draw from reports of the champion's sudden illness. The evidence of Renforth's companions, both at the inquest and on their return to England, is clear in rejecting the theory that he had suffered a fit, and, incidentally, provides background information on the pattern of Renforth's fitting.

James Percy, Joseph Walton and William Oldham all seem to have been familiar with Renforth's fitting behaviour, and none of the three recognised his symptoms as being at all similar to one of his fits. Typically it appears that Renforth would have a fit after a race, when he was excited and had taken a drink. Walton, who had known Renforth well for five years, said he was only aware of Renforth having four fits during that time. It seems that Renforth had true *grand mal* fits, losing consciousness and control of his limbs, which meant that he would not have been able to continue rowing in the way that he had for several hundred yards. The seizures occurred quite infrequently, which is what one would expect of a man who had first pursued a career as a swimmer before turning to the tricky business of rowing unstable skiffs and racing shells. Renforth would have drowned long before reaching the top of his profession if he had suffered frequent fits.

Further questioning of Percy and Kelley concentrated on whether or not Renforth was under stress at the time of his collapse. Both men were adamant that the boat had moved smoothly off the start, was soon in the lead and that no extra effort had even been thought of before Kelley had asked Renforth for 'a dozen'. The English crew had expected to win and up to the point of Renforth's collapse they had remained confident that they would do so. Any stress that Renforth had appeared under to spectators was the result of his 'attack' rather than the cause of it. Renforth had rowed in many big races without the pressure of the occasion getting to him in the slightest degree.

A letter in the *Newcastle Daily Chronicle* (see following page) of Monday 28th August added to the debate over the cause of Renforth's death.

It is possible that Joseph Walton was aware of Surgeon Bell's views, since he had asked at the post mortem for the heart to be removed in order that it could undergo further examination. The heart was healthy, showing that Surgeon Bell's diagnosis of hypertrophy (enlargement) was mistaken. The fit that Renforth had after his race with Bright, which had been reported in the newspapers of the time, was typical in that it had occurred after a race and when he had taken drink. The evidence of lack of pulse is interesting, but since Bell had been proved wrong with the diagnosis of heart disease, it appeared fruitless to pursue his views further.

## THE DEATH OF RENFORTH.

### TO THE EDITOR OF THE DAILY CHRONICLE.

SIR,—Before definite information reaches this country as to the cause of the death of poor Renforth, it may possibly tend to allay the apprehension of his relatives and friends as to foul play having been used, if I state that on one occasion I was called to attend him while suffering from a fit on the evening of his race with Bright. I found him exceedingly ill, pulseless, and cold, and he had three successive epileptic fits in my presence. From the examination I then made I came to the conclusion that he was suffering from hypertrophy of the heart, and advised his friends to get him to discontinue rowing. The symptoms described of his late sudden illness would, in my opinion, quite account for his death having arisen from natural causes—the condition of his heart and the fact of his being predisposed to epileptiform convulsions. After the first shock of the melancholy news—for no one shared more deeply in the universal regret at the untimely end of our gallant oarsman—I could not but recall the symptoms of his case upon that occasion when I visited him at the Belted Will Inn. Admiring the noble fellow for his skill and enduring pluck, yet I always greatly dreaded the sad termination that has caused so much sorrowing in every Tyneside home.—I remain, yours faithfully.          ANTHONY BELL, surgeon.

6, Eldon Square, Newcastle, Aug. 26, 1871.

Other suggestions were made in the American press that it was Renforth's stringent training regime that had undermined his health. Always an attractive opinion when placed before readers who are likely to be sitting down, and might even be drinking and smoking as they sagely consider the news!

Frankly it was baffling. How could an athlete at the peak of his powers be struck down in this way with no apparent cause? Renforth's muscular strength and endurance had proved so much greater than his rivals that challenges for single sculls, pair oar races, and even four oar contests, were frequently made 'bar Renforth'. A pathologist, writing in the *Newcastle Daily Chronicle* of Thursday 5th October 1871 to contradict a view expressed in the *Newcastle Daily Journal* that Renforth had hypertrophy of the heart, showed that some people realised at the time that death sometimes occurred suddenly, and without explanation.

> **Any medical man, however, who has conducted a large number of post mortem examinations has occasionally met with cases in which no changes can be detected to account for death. Perhaps poor Renforth might have ranked amongst these.**

There remained a body of opinion that Renforth had been got at it some way, probably with poison, but the matter remained a mystery until comparatively recently when the medical profession began to study the small number of people who die suddenly for no apparent reason. These studies showed that those who have epilepsy, and have seizures, are at greater risk from this phenomenon than the rest of the population.

This phenomenon, of death without apparent organic cause, has been given the name 'sudden unexplained death'. Unusually for a death of this period, because of his fame and the circumstances under which he died, it is possible to draw parallels between Renforth's death and the conclusions of recent medical, statistical and pathological studies of 'sudden unexplained death'.

Firstly, it is now believed that cardiac arrhythmias (irregular heartbeat) is one of the most common risk factors facing young people with epilepsy. This accords with Surgeon Bell's finding no pulse when called to attend Renforth in Newcastle and also with the failure of Renforth to bleed when veins were opened in his arms to try to encourage circulation after his collapse in Canada. Evidence has been collected to show that stress is a factor in arrhythmias and although Renforth was apparently calm and not under great physical pressure at the start of the race, the mental strain of stroking the boat in such an important contest will have put him under some stress. Once he had begun to suffer the stress would have been enormous, since he was well aware of the great expectations of his supporters. Hence his remark to Walton, while he was on his deathbed, 'What will they say at home?'

Secondly, data from the Cook County (USA) Coroner's office indicates that the risk of sudden death in epilepsy may approach 1 in 200 persons in the general epilepsy population. If the population assessed is that of males between 20 and 40 years with symptomatic epilepsy – a profile that accords with the 29 year old Renforth – the risk of sudden death may exceed 1 in 50.

Thirdly, pathological observations at post mortem of victims of sudden unexplained death in epilepsy, although by definition unrevealing as to an immediate cause, do provide an associated finding which is helpful in comparisons with other sudden deaths.

Haemorrhagic pulmonary oedema (congestion) is commonly, but not universally found in the lungs of victims. This is what was found at the post mortem on Renforth and it provides corroboratory evidence that he also was a victim of sudden unexplained death.

One hesitates to come to a definite conclusion about Renforth's death so long after the event, especially when some of his friends and sections of the press remained unconvinced by the natural causes explanation. However, they were nearly all gambling men and one suspects that the odds drawn from the statistics gathered by the Cook County Coroner's office would have impressed them. A greater

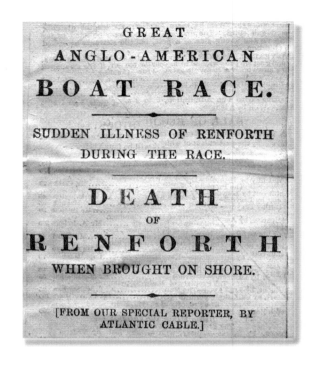

GREAT
ANGLO-AMERICAN
BOAT RACE.

SUDDEN ILLNESS OF RENFORTH
DURING THE RACE.

DEATH
OF
RENFORTH
WHEN BROUGHT ON SHORE.

[FROM OUR SPECIAL REPORTER, BY
ATLANTIC CABLE.]

than 1 in 50 chance that their star oarsman and stroke would die suddenly would certainly have made them circumspect about offering odds of 2 to 1 on a victory for Renforth's crew. The weight of evidence seems to point to death from natural causes – 'sudden unexplained death' as a complication of epilepsy.

Renforth's body was swiftly embalmed to preserve it for the journey back to Tyneside. It was decided that the champion's remains should be sent home as soon as possible. William Oldham was charged with accompanying the coffin across the Atlantic on the steam packet *Nova Scotian*, which was due to leave Halifax on Saturday 26th August 1871.

The body was then conveyed from St John to the champion's house in James Street, Gateshead, with all the solemnity, deference and show that characterised the Victorian way of death.

At Halifax the transfer from the coastal steamer to the *Nova Scotian* became a fully-fledged procession of mourners. The rival English crew of Taylor, Winship, Sadler and Bagnall followed the body in its triple coffin and external packing case. They were joined by English employees of the Nova Scotia railway, and others, in paying their final respects to Renforth.

A swift passage to Liverpool was followed by the train journey to Tyneside where the body was taken off the train at Gateshead for its penultimate journey to the champion's house. Eight former workmates of Renforth from his days working on the demolition of the Tyne Bridge were chosen to be bearers of the body. After the coffin had been transferred to a hearse it made its solemn way up the hill to James Street. Even the street urchins, usually completely lacking in decorum, could only find it in their hearts to whistle the *Dead March*. When the house was reached, the coffin was taken out of its case and those present were able to cast their eyes on the champion's face through a plate glass window set into the coffin lid. This proved all too much for the young widow, who broke down in utter distress and desolation when confronted with the remains of her husband.

Nobody had imagined that Renforth would return to Gateshead in his coffin. Tyneside had buried two of its rowing heroes, Bob Chambers and Harry Clasper in the past few years. Now it would give the youngest to die, and arguably the greatest, of the Tyne oarsmen the send off which his fame deserved.

# Funeral, Memorial and Legacy

The viewing of Renforth's face through the window in the coffin by friends and family of the champion seems to have awakened a thought in somebody's mind that it might be possible to turn a profit from allowing members of the public to do the same. The *Gateshead Observer*, always better for gossip than its Newcastle counterparts, reported the story in its edition of 9th September 1871.

**Poor Renforth will be buried tomorrow. We understand that some of the relations of the deceased have been advised to allow the general public to view the features of the late champion at *sixpence a head* (!), the money to be given to the widow. We need scarcely say that so base and uncharitable proposition has been met in a proper spirit by the deceased's friends, who have indignantly refused to countenance any such proceeding. They may rest assured that money will be plentiful, and the widow will be provided for.**

The separation of 'friends' from 'relations' is significant. Renforth had successfully transcended his lowly social status not only to perform well on the river but also to be accepted and respected by the publicans and businessmen who ran professional rowing. As events unfolded after his death, the split between his relations, and in particular his widow, and his rowing friends becomes increasingly apparent. For the moment, having averted the threat of the dead champion's face being made available for gawping at by anybody prepared to pay sixpence to do so, arrangements for the interment of the body were able to proceed.

Renforth was to be buried on Sunday 10th September 1871, at 2.30pm in St Edmund's Cemetery, Gateshead. The funeral procession would start from the champion's James Street home, with a large crowd expected to accompany the hearse on its journey to the cemetery. The grave chosen for Renforth was to be directly opposite the resting place of his father.

By noon on Sunday thousands of people had made their way to Gateshead. At two o'clock the coffin was lifted into the glass-sided hearse and draped with a Union Jack. Wreaths of flowers, a Free Masons apron which had belonged to the late champion Bob Chambers, and a Free Gardeners scarf, were placed on top of the covering Union flag. Renforth was a member of Newcastle's St Peter's Masonic Lodge and also a member of the United Order of Free Gardeners. James Street was packed with people anxious to take part in the procession and it was about half past two before a move was made. The funeral procession formed up in the following order:

Members of the Ancient Order of Free Masons, four abreast.
Members of local rowing clubs, four abreast.
Members of local swimming clubs, four abreast.
The Newcastle and Gateshead Operatic Band of about sixty performers.
Four mutes – Mr Edward Winship, Mr John Martin, Mr Robert Cooper, and Mr H B Cave.
The hearse containing the body, drawn by four horses.
Relatives of the deceased, four abreast.
Supporters, backers, and personal friends of the deceased, four abreast.
Members of the United Order of Free Gardeners, four abreast.
Band of the 1st Durham (Jarrow) Volunteer Engineers.
Members of other friendly societies, four abreast.
The general public, four abreast.

The solemn procession passed through Gateshead, along Heaton Terrace, Mulgrave Terrace, and Hill Street, into High Street on its way to the cemetery. Thousands packed the route as the bands played the *Dead March in Saul*. The crowd was estimated to have been between 70,000 and 100,000 people. It took the hearse an hour-and-a-half to reach the cemetery, the extremely slow pace being principally due to the crowded state of the streets. Orders had been given that only those who were part of the procession should be allowed to enter the burial ground but it proved impossible to maintain control. Thousands climbed the external railings and walls and pressed against the barricading placed around the open grave. Amazingly nobody was injured in the crush as men, women and boys rushed forward to satisfy their morbid curiosity.

Once the coffin had been lowered into its final resting place and the funeral rites had been performed, numerous bouquets of flowers were thrown into the grave by friends and relations of the champion. After a final glance at the coffin the crowd dispersed and within a few hours Gateshead had returned to normal. Despite the huge crowd and the unseemly scaling of the cemetery railings, no accidents were reported. During the funeral, bells were tolled in St Nicholas's Church, Newcastle and St Mary's, Gateshead, and afterwards the ringers of St Mary's rang a funeral peal.

When the news of Renforth's death reached Tyneside there had been immediate speculation as to what provision the champion might have made for his wife and child. At first newspaper reports had been upbeat. They were sure that Renforth would have saved a sufficient sum, at least four hundred guineas, to provide for his family. He was recognised to have been a man of steady habits who had recently become a member of several building societies. Two weeks later the tone had changed somewhat. Renforth had been commendably provident and had not left his dependents entirely destitute, but it should not be forgotten that he was still very young. Therefore he had not had the opportunity of saving what could be considered a sufficiency for his wife and child.

Even before the funeral had taken place, Renforth's friends were determined to raise sufficient funds to fulfil a three-fold purpose. They wished to defray the expenses of the burial, to raise a memorial stone over the grave, and to establish a fund for the benefit of the champion's widow and daughter.

Many prominent citizens subscribed directly to the Renforth Memorial Fund and a series of events was also planned. Memorial concerts were held all over the North East at which the two crews who had recently returned from Canada often appeared on stage in their American rowing costume. Just as each of the champion's great victories had been marked with the composition of a popular song, so his death was similarly commemorated. During a memorial concert at Gateshead Town Hall on 11th October 1871, Joe Wilson performed a newly-written song which reflected the sense of loss felt by Tynesiders when the news of Renforth's death had first reached Newcastle.

### THE DEETH O' RENFORTH!
### CHAMPION SCULLER OF THE WORLD

YE cruel Atlantic Cable,
What's myed ye bring such fearful news?
When Tyneside's hardly yeble
Such sudden grief te bide.
Hoo me heart it beats, – iv'rybody greets,
As the whisper runs throo dowley streets,
'We've lost poor Jimmy Renforth,
The Champein o' Tyneside!'

Hoo sad, hoo unexpected,
What diff'rent news we thowt te hear,
Till dismay'd an' affected,
Heart-broken mourners cried,
'Jimmy Renforth's gyen, wor greet Champein's gyen,
Iv a country strange, away frae hyem,
We've lost poor Jimmy Renforth,
The Champein o'Tyneside!'

Oh, Jim, what myed ye leave us?
What myed ye leave the canny toon?
A journey myed to grieve us,
Ye've gyen wi' the last tide,
An' the oar that fell, the last oar that fell
Frae yor helpless hand, just seem'd te tell
That Deeth wes the greet victor
I' races far an' wide!

Life lost withoot a warnin,
An' stopt yor short but grand koreer,
Then left us stricken, mournin,
Deprived o' wor greet pride;
Hoo me heart it beats, – iv'rybody greets,
As the whisper runs throo dowley streets,
'We've lost poor Jimmy Renforth,
The Champein o' Tyneside!'

Joe Wilson soon worked up another song about Renforth's death to perform around the music halls, in which he hailed Renforth as the best of all the aquatic champions.

### THE CHAMPEIN OV ALL CHAMPEINS.
### AS SUNG BY THE AUTHOR IN THE MUSIC HALLS

*(TEUN- 'Babylon is Falling.')*

I' THE bloom o' life he left us,
Wi' thowts o' nowt but vict'ry,
He cross'd the greet Atlantic wiv his crew;
Nivvor dreamin o' misfortin,
Till Deeth's dreed visitation
Struck helpless the grand fellow that we knew.

*Korus.*

*Gyen frae the hyem we knaw he liked se weel!*
*Gyen frae the frinds that held him ivor dear!*
*We've lost poor Jimmy Renforth,*
*The Champein ov all Champeins,*
*The hero of all rivers, far an' near.*

Wiv a crew byeth brave an' manly,
The frinds that he had fancied,
He started on a journey myed te pain,
An' bring sorrow, sad an' weary,
Te hearts that least expected
They'd hear a bard gie vent i' mournful strain.
*Gyen frae the hyem etc.*

Oh! Jim, what myed ye leave us?
What myed ye leave the Tyneside
Te meet yor deeth se sadly, far away?
An' hearts wes fairly broken,
Te hear thor gallant Champein,
I' Harry Kelley's airms, se lifeless lay.
*Gyen frae the hyem etc.*

Ye cruel Atlantic Cable,
What fearful news ye browt us,
What different tidings we expected here;
Till dismay'd an' affected,
We heard a fearful whisper
Run throo the toon like leetnin, far an' near
*Gyen frae the hyem etc.*

This completed the cycle of songs that Joe Wilson had written about Renforth, although that is not to say that the late champion's spirit could not be invoked at a later date in other songs! In *If Deed Foaks com te life Agyen!* Wilson imagined the ghost of Renforth saying, 'Is Tynside men te let Joe Sadler rest alyen? It's time aw wes alive agyen, If ye cannet find a reet un!' This was in response to the London sculler's domination of the rowing scene in the aftermath of Renforth's death.

On the day of the Gateshead concert the fund stood at £317 13s 0d and a further £26 10s was raised that night. The fund continued to swell and was declared closed at the end of January 1872 when over £500 had been collected. At the same meeting of the committee various designs for a memorial stone were considered, and one from the sculptor George Burn, of the Neville Arcade, Newcastle was chosen. Burn was very much in practice at carrying out this type of commission since it was he who had executed the memorials of both Harry Clasper and Bob Chambers. While Burn set to work on the sculpture the committee proceeded with other business and was able to present accounts in March.

Total subscriptions received, £534 9s 7d. Against this, £80 16s 5d for the funeral expenses, bringing home the corpse etc., £33 12s 1d for working expenses of getting subscriptions, printing, stationery, stamps etc., £50 cost of monument. Total expenditure, £164 8s 6d. A balance of £370 1s 1d was thus left to be appropriated for the benefit of the champion's widow and child.

However relations between the committee and the widow had not proceeded smoothly. On 20th December 1871 Mary Renforth was asked to attend the committee meeting because rumours were circulating that she was destitute, having received only £1 6s since the death of her husband. Reading between the lines of the newspaper report the following day it appears that the committee was fairly certain that the rumour had its origins with her. She was brought before the committee to make an emphatic denial that she was destitute and to admit that she had received over £100. This admission is slightly puzzling since one would have expected that the payments to the widow would have appeared in the accounts, which they do not. One can only assume that payments to her were made privately, presumably from the pockets of members of the committee, or their friends.

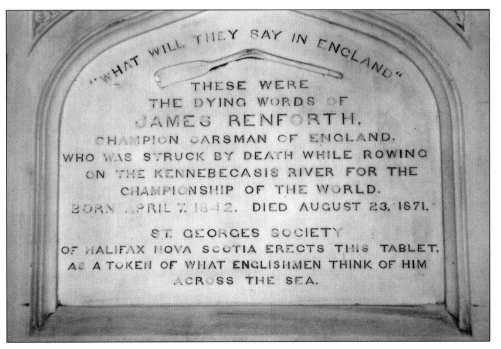

*The memorial of Nova Scotian marble which remains in place at the west end of the former St Mary's Church, Gateshead, beside the Tyne Bridge.*

There was also trouble over the sign for the Sir Charles Napier Inn. It appears that Renforth, who had sold the pub to a Mr J.T. Fisher prior to going into serious training for his 1871 Canadian campaign, had been unhappy before leaving Tyneside that Mr Fisher was continuing to trade under his (Renforth's) sign. The sign must have said something like, 'Sir Charles Napier Inn – The house of the sculling champion of the world, James Renforth'. Fisher claimed that the sign was part of the fixtures and fittings of the public house and as such he was entitled to keep and do with it what he liked. The family were demanding it back, possibly to auction for the benefit of the Memorial Fund. Mr Fisher was determined to hang on to the sign, and said so in a letter to the *Newcastle Daily Chronicle* of 10th October 1871, although he did offer to make a generous contribution to the Fund. For the moment at least a temporary, if disputed, memorial to the champion continued to hang outside his former place of business.

A memorial of a more conventional nature in the form of a carved stone tablet was sent from Canada by the St George's Society of Halifax, Nova Scotia. Made of Nova Scotian marble, it was set into the wall of the baptistry of St Mary's Church, Gateshead, the Renforths' parish church. It has a simple central design of a broken oar, representative of life taken away prematurely, and includes a paraphrase of one of

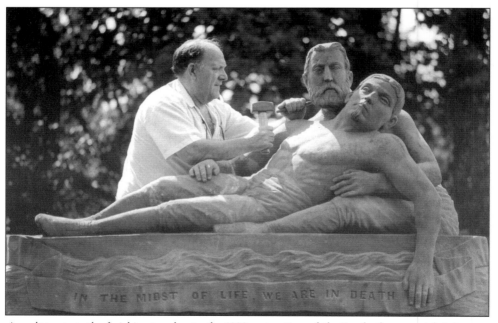

*Ted Ditchburn: North News & Pictures*

*A sculptor puts the finishing touches to the 1992 restoration of the Renforth memorial. It is now sited in Prince Consort Road, Gateshead, outside the Shipley Art Gallery.*

Renforth's last utterances, 'What will they say in England'. The marble tablet remains in place today where it seems modest and understated in comparison with the massive sandstone block out of which Burn carved his image of events on the Kennebeccasis River.

On 28th October 1872, the grave memorial was inaugurated in St Edmund's Cemetery, Gateshead. Mindful of the chaotic scenes that had accompanied Renforth's funeral, the Cemetery Committee had requested that there be no public demonstration at the ceremony, so only a small group gathered to witness proceedings. After a short speech by Mr Pickett, the sculptor was asked to unveil the monument, which up to now had been shrouded with a Union Jack. Over time critics have been less than kind about George Burn's work – one of his other statues is described in Pevsner as 'perhaps the funniest monument in the County' (Durham) and by another observer as resembling a giant garden gnome – but contemporary opinion of his memorial to Renforth was very favourable.

*Ian Whitehead*

*A commemorative dinner plate manufactured by Thomas Fell of St Peter's, Newcastle upon Tyne, after the death of Renforth in 1871.*

The Renforth memorial is wholly executed in Prudham stone, and is 11 feet 6 inches high by 8 feet long at the base. It is about 14 tons in weight, and parallelogram in form. It is composed of three basement courses, carved on which are three rampant lions representing England, and seven stars of America, giving an international character to the design. On the basement is placed a large die with an inscription as follows:-

'Erected by public subscription, to the memory of James Renforth of Gateshead, champion sculler of the World, who died August 23rd, 1871, aged 29 years, while rowing in an international boat race between the English and American crews, on the Kennebeccasis River, near St John, N.B.'

Above the inscription block is placed a sarcophagus, surrounded with wreaths of bay and oak leaves, emblems of victory. On the front and back is sculptured the life-sized medallion of James Percy and Robert Chambers, the latter being a very good likeness. The monument is surmounted by the historic group of Renforth falling into the arms of Kelley in the boat, and faithfully depicts the melancholy incident so fully described at the time; and which is further enforced by the ribbon scroll carved round the boat, and is inscribed with the appropriate text, "In the midst of life we are in death." The whole design of the monument shows great simplicity and massiveness, and is in keeping with the character of the late champion. The figures are a careful study of nature as shown by the relaxed muscles and fading expression of consciousness of Renforth. The intensity of seriousness and wonder, as well as the fine, manly vigour of form in Kelley, give great force and character to the work, and will convey to the public a good moral lesson on the uncertainty of human life.

*Gateshead Observer* 2nd November 1872

'Frigger' in the form of a glass egg and stand to commemorate James Renforth, and an unknown man and his dog.

For myself I have to say that my first impression that the sculptor had been overly melodramatic in his portrayal has been tempered by the knowledge that he has shown Renforth falling back into Kelley's arms, exactly as it happened. Readers who are able to visit the memorial must make up their own minds, but I have grown rather fond of the work.

The memorial remained in the cemetery until the mid 1980s, when, after repeated vandalism, Gateshead Council removed it to storage until a less vulnerable site could be found. Eventually it was restored and resited in August 1992 outside the Shipley Art Gallery, Gateshead, where it remains today.

Other material tokens of remembrance, for purchase by individuals, were produced at the time of Renforth's death. Portraits of the champion went on sale from a Newcastle Engravers: one 21 inches by 17 inches cost 3s 6d, one 9 inches by 6 inches cost 4d, and a 6 inches by 4½ inches version was only one penny. The pottery of Thomas Fell at St Peter's, Newcastle, produced commemorative ware with a transfer printed head and shoulders portrait of the champion on each piece. A unique memorial piece which is in the possession of Tyne and Wear Museums is a glass 'frigger' – a piece of work produced by a glass blower to demonstrate his skill – in the form of a large glass 'egg' on a stand. The egg has a photographic portrait of the champion mounted on its inside surface and the whole rather garish assemblage is painted pink and blue, also on the inside surface, to represent the colours of the St John and English crews.

One genuine relic of the occasion of Renforth's death can be found in Beamish Museum's collection. It is Renforth's flannel bodyshirt, which he stripped off just before the race. The shirt is mounted in a period glass case with a label explaining its origins and has obviously been displayed prior to its entry into Beamish, perhaps in a pub. A Renforth relative has informed me that it was once on display at Newcastle Central Station. The shirt is sleeveless with faded blue piping around the four-button neck, and the arm holes. The initials 'J R' have been roughly marked on the material in

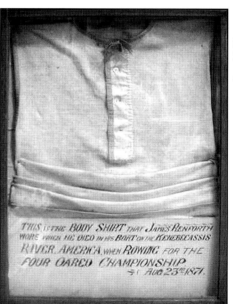

Beamish Museum

THIS IS THE BODY SHIRT THAT JAMES RENFORTH WORE WHEN HE DIED IN HIS BOAT ON THE KENEBECASSIS RIVER AMERICA WHEN ROWING FOR THE FOUR OARED CHAMPIONSHIP AUG 23RD 1871.

*Renforth's shirt from August 1871.*

141

ink, no doubt for laundry purposes.

The most significant memorial is not in England at all, but in Canada. When a resort village sprang up on the banks of the Kennebeccasis River at the end of the 19th century its residents decided it should take the name of 'Renforth'. And so it became in October 1903, with official colours of pink and blue to represent the colours of the two crews in the fateful race. Renforth is now a district of St John, but the name lives on.

Renforth's funeral made a huge impression on Tyneside, and was reported across the world, but memory of such an event quickly fades. His memorial stone had to be moved to protect it from attacks by vandals, probably unaware of his great sporting achievements as well as uncaring of the sanctity of the burial ground. He left little in the way of material wealth to sustain his widow and young daughter. The question then arises: did his short but hugely successful rowing career have any lasting effect on the sport? Renforth was no Harry Clasper, who defined the basic shape of the rowing shell and produced the first practical outrigger, but I believe that he did play a part in the development and early adoption of the sliding seat. It is something of a paradox since he never used a sliding seat: all his victories were gained in fixed seat boats.

As early as the 1850s Harry Clasper and his brothers were sliding on their seats to give extra length and power to their stroke. To use the sliding motion an oarsman had to sit low in the boat, straighten his legs during the stroke by driving off the footboard, and perhaps most importantly, have his feet firmly strapped to the board so he could pull himself forward at the end of the stroke. This technique contrasted with that of sitting still on the seat, with almost all movement, and most power, coming from above the waist. The sliding on the seat technique quickly became identified as the 'traditional Tyne stroke', but even on the Tyne some rowers slid hardly at all, while others, as contemporary reports put it, 'made good use of the footboard'. Bob Cooper, 'the Redheugh ferryman', rowed at a high tempo which did not allow for full use of the legs, while the great sculler Bob Chambers, a protégé of Harry Clasper, made considerable use of his legs to row a long powerful stroke.

There were a number of attempts to develop a sliding seat in the 1860s. Walter Brown, the American sculler who later beat William Sadler on the Tyne in 1869, tried one in 1861. A Dr Schiller of Berlin made a slide using small wheels in 1863, but nobody achieved sufficient success to encourage the best oarsmen to switch away from fixed seat rowing.

Indeed at this time there was not a general acceptance that sliding was superior to sitting still. Followers of rowing could see the benefits of the extra power and length of stroke but weighed those against the effect on the 'run' or momentum of the boat when the oarsman pulled his weight towards the stern to get in position to take his next stroke. After Henry Kelley of Putney, who sat still on his seat, defeated the North's beloved Bob Chambers in 1865, those who favoured the straight-backed, non-sliding technique could justifiably claim that their method was as good as, or better than, the sliding technique developed on the Tyne.

The arrival of Renforth on the scene quickly began to alter opinion. At first observers declared his stroke ugly – The *Daily Telegraph* dubbed him the 'Radical' oarsman – but they soon recognised the great effectiveness of his technique. His unbroken string of victories in all boats – single sculls, pairs and fours – forced the pundits to accept that Renforth's stroke was better for winning races than the seemingly more stylish techniques employed by his opponents.

A reporter writing for *Bell's Life* after Renforth's victory over Kelley in November 1868 put it like this:

> One very notable feature of his style is the great use he makes of his legs; indeed, we have no hesitation in saying that we never met with a sculler, not even excepting the late Bob Chambers who so fully understood the important art of bringing every muscle together with the full weight of the body to bear on every stroke; and we are satisfied that this is the great secret of his wonderful turn of speed, which enabled him to vanquish such a 'flier' as Kelley.

Having run out of opponents willing to take him on in single sculls, Renforth increasingly rowed as stroke oar in pairs and fours. Men who came into his boat had to adapt to his style. John Martin, recruited from the Pelaw Main Trimmers crew to row in the engine-room of the Champion Four in 1869, began awkwardly because of his upright style. He soon adjusted to Renforth's stroke and was a successful member of the Champion Four until the split between Taylor and Renforth at the end of the 1870 season. Even Harry Kelley, to whom Renforth turned when Martin and Winship threw their lot in with Taylor after the argument at Lachine, changed his stroke to fit in with the champion. The Tyne-Thames pairing comprehensively dismantled Winship and Taylor when the showdown race took place in January 1871. Subsequently Kelley continued to row very successfully at 3, directly behind Renforth, in the four which the champion took to Canada in 1871.

Renforth's dominance had its effect on those who were trying to develop a successful sliding seat. The campaign in North America in 1870 and the victory at Lachine seem to have influenced the Americans, and in particular J.C. Babcock of the Nassau Rowing Club of New York, a champion oarsman and sculler. Babcock had experimented with a slide in 1857 but did not consider it a success. In 1870 he tried again and this time was pleased with the results that he obtained with a trained crew. Novices however, found it more difficult than fixed seat rowing.

Babcock's slide used a seat which was a 10 inch-square wooden frame covered with leather and grooved at the edges to slide on two brass tracks fastened on the thwart, allowing a slide of 10-12 inches. The tracks were lubricated with lard and gave a 'rowing' length of slide of up to 6 inches. Babcock wrote a letter about the slide to Waters Balch on 14 December 1870 which shows how Renforth's 1870 crew was influencing his thinking. It concludes:

> **The slide properly used is a decided advantage and gain of speed, and the only objection to its use is its complication and almost impracticable requirement of skill and unison in a crew, rather than any defect in its mechanical theory. When we take into consideration that the best oarsmen in the world, the Tynesiders, slide, when spirting, from four to six inches on a fixed seat, the moveable seat can only be considered as a mechanical contrivance, intended for a better accomplishment of the sliding movement in rowing.**

By 1871 American professionals were successfully using slides of the Babcock type in races, notably at Saratoga, and at Halifax, Nova Scotia, where they competed against Winship's crew and Chambers's crew, which was made up of the remaining four from Renforth's crew. The Biglin crew competed using slides at Saratoga in both the fours and the sculls races. They did not win, but then neither did either of the English crews. Ironically the fours race was won by the Ward brothers, rowing in *Dunston-on-Tyne*, the Jewitt-built boat in which Renforth's crew had triumphed at Lachine the previous year.

After competing in regattas at Saratoga, Longueil, Halifax and Quebec, the two predominantly Tyneside crews – Joe Sadler was the Londoner in Winship's crew, and of course Harry Kelley rowed in the Chambers crew – returned to England. They received great receptions, with an estimated 10,000 people turning out to greet the Chambers crew at Newcastle, and hostilities resumed almost immediately. A four-oared race for £400 was set to take place on the Tyne on Wednesday 22nd November and both crews went back into training. The races in North America had not conclusively proved which was the better of the two. The only way to decide was in the traditional manner, with a match over the Tyne Championship course.

When the two crews appeared at the start the Winship four, rather surprisingly, were rowing with slides. These were identical to those of American design they had encountered across the Atlantic, except that they had front and back stops to prevent the seat from becoming detached from the slide. The crew had only used them for the

*Bob Bagnall's sliding seat from the November 1871 race on the Tyne against the remaining members of Renforth's crew.*

first time the day before the race but they had obviously concluded that the risk of using the sliding seats was worth taking, despite their lack of practice with them. One detects the hand of James Taylor, the inveterate experimenter, in the decision to row with slides but there is no mention in the race report that he was behind this bold choice.

Robert Bagnall, then aged 22 and, following the death of Renforth, the best Tyneside sculler in training, rowed behind Winship at 3. The seat and slide which he used in this historic race is in the collection of Tyne and Wear Museums at the Newcastle Discovery Museum.

In the event they won the race, completing the destruction of the former Renforth crew and ensuring that oarsmen throughout Britain would swiftly adopt the use of sliding seats. Tynesiders had been sliding *on* their seats since the 1850s, but henceforth they would be sliding *with* their seats. They could also look forward to less trouble with boils on their buttocks – something that Percy had suffered from in the run-up to this race.

The *Newcastle Daily Chronicle* of Thursday November 23rd 1871 put it thus in its conclusion to the race report:

> **The result of this contest will most probably be the adoption of the sliding seat, at least in fours, and perhaps in pairs and skiffs as well.**

Although this reflects a rather Tynecentric view of the rowing world, the success of Renforth and his companions over the previous three years did seem to justify opinions such as these.

The development of a practical slide is quite rightly assigned to Babcock. However Renforth's success with a stroke which manifestly involved sliding considerably, albeit on a seat rather than with a slide, encouraged Babcock and his contemporaries to press on with their experiments. Renforth was so dominant after November 1868 that his technique was bound to be recognised as providing exceptional extra power from the legs. Renforth has no claim on the invention of the slide but Babcock's letter, acknowledging that the Tynesiders were the best oarsmen in the world, and that he was only trying to achieve mechanically what they did when they slid on their seats, shows the influence that Renforth and his crews had on Babcock's thinking. The slide would have come eventually but Renforth's rowing legacy must be the general adoption of it for race rowing so soon after his death.

THE LATE JAMES RENFORTH,
Champion Sculler of England.

*Portrait of Renforth sold as a souvenir at one of the late summer regattas held in North America after the tragedy at St John.*

# Epilogue

On Monday 19th May 1884 at Newcastle County Court, an action was brought before Mr D. Bradshaw by the widow and daughter of the late James Renforth, the champion sculler, against the trustees of the fund which had been raised by public subscription and had been set apart for the benefit of Renforth's daughter.

The original trustees had been Thomas Pickett, Joshua Bagnall, John Elliott and William Blakey; all prominent figures on the Tyneside rowing scene, with connections to James Renforth's career. Pickett died in 1876 and was followed by Blakey in 1880. Initially Blakey's widow had been named as a defendant, as the administrator of her husband's estate, but when it was revealed that his debts had consumed all of his assets her name was struck out by consent of all parties. John Elliott, who was Chief Constable of Gateshead, and Joshua Bagnall, who you may recall had owned the Oxford Music Hall, were thus left to defend the case.

The plaintiffs were John Heler and Ann Elizabeth, his wife, the daughter of James Renforth, and William John Renforth (James's cousin) and Mary Ann, his wife, who previous to her second marriage had been the widow of James Renforth. There were legal arguments to be settled about whether or not the Memorial Committee had created a trust, and if it had, whether or not the defendants had been made aware that they had become trustees. However, these issues were largely addressed by referring to how the defendants had dealt with the money which had been left in the Memorial Fund after the cost of the memorial sculpture and other expenses had been met. The balance in the fund at that time was £370 1s 1d. A meeting was called in April 1872 at which it was decided to pay £170 to the widow, leaving £200 in the fund. Four trustees were appointed, Messrs. Pickett, Blakey, Bagnall and Elliott, and the decision made that the remaining £200 should be invested, at interest, in their names for the benefit of the orphaned daughter, Ann Elizabeth. The April meeting passed a resolution that until the orphan was 17 years of age the £200 should be held by the Tyne Commission, when, if they thought fit, the trustees might give her the principal. Neither Elliott nor Bagnall was present at this meeting.

The Memorial Fund money had been held in Lambton's Bank and the £200 remained there until March 1873, when the trustees had paid both the interest and the principal – a total of £206 12s 5d – into the Northern Counties Bank. Despite the decision taken at the April 1872 meeting of the Memorial Committee, the money was at no time invested with the Tyne Commission. It was not until July 1881 that Joshua Bagnall told Mrs Renforth that the move to the Northern Counties Bank was made to obtain better interest. Joshua Bagnall had taken the leading role in looking after the money, collecting the interest and paying it to Mrs Renforth at six-monthly intervals until 1881 when the payments stopped, because the Northern Counties Bank had failed. Ann Elizabeth, Renforth's daughter, was 17 on 21st December 1880.

Renforth's widow and daughter both gave evidence, the daughter saying that she had seen in the papers that the Northern Counties bank was paying out 3s 6d in the pound, which suggests that she was able to read. Officials of Lambton's and the Northern Counties Banks were also called to the witness stand. The manager of the Northern Counties Bank told the court that Joshua Bagnall was a shareholder and a considerable debtor to the bank. Bagnall's motives in switching the Memorial Fund money to a bank in which he had an interest, and to which he owed money, must be doubted at the very least.

The case was also complicated by the paternalistic attitudes of the day. Renforth's daughter had married very young and there was some doubt about what would happen if she was paid the money and then became destitute before she reached the age of 21. The trustees, and the bank, were reluctant to pay out the money in case either John Heler, the husband, or Mary Renforth, the mother, got their hands on it. Bagnall clearly had his own commercial and personal reasons for retaining the money in the bank, but Elliott had nothing to gain.

When Elliott was called to give evidence he twisted and turned to try and avoid responsibility as a trustee, and it is impossible not to feel some sympathy for him. Bagnall had been the acting trustee and Elliott had countersigned cheques as requested but had not really been involved in the administration of the fund once the funeral had taken place. Elliott had not fully realised the legal implications of accepting responsibility, as one of a group of individuals, for the remaining £200.

In giving evidence Elliott tried to show that he would not have accepted a trusteeship because of his personal animosity towards Renforth's widow. He said that he had told the late Edward Winship that he would not be a trustee for Mrs Renforth. He had seen her going about in a brake (horse-drawn bus) drunk while Renforth was in

*A horse-drawn bus on Blackett Street, Newcastle, around 1900.*

Canada and in such a state as he objected to. He had expected that some of the money would have gone to the child, but he would not have been in favour of the widow getting any.

Elliott and Bagnall's barrister, Mr Strachan, attempted to assert that no trust had been formed and, even if it had, the defendants had not been told that they had become trustees, but he was interrupted by the judge. Mr Bradshaw remarked that he found for the plaintiffs with costs, but that the defendants had the option of an appeal if they chose to take advantage of it.

The case supplies a sad postscript to the wonderful rowing career of James Renforth. But, fortuitously, it also allows us to take a closer look at some of the key figures involved with Renforth in his home and sporting life. William Blakey and Joshua Bagnall, the principal backers of the two schools of Tyne professional rowing are ultimately revealed as business failures. Blakey died in 1880 leaving his widow with debts greater than his assets. Bagnall made dubious use of the Memorial Fund money, investing it in a bank of which he was a shareholder, and to which he owed money, in contravention of the resolution to put it with the Tyne Commission. Although

Bagnall's current financial position was not made clear during the case, he does not appear to have had any funds available to replace even part of the lost £200.

The animosity of John Elliott to Mary Ann Renforth confirms absolutely the hostility which Renforth's rowing friends appeared to show towards his widow in the first few months after his death. Elliott was trying to get himself out of trouble but his testimony about Mary Renforth and her behaviour seems heartfelt. A *Newcastle Daily Chronicle* editorial about Renforth in the immediate aftermath of the tragedy in Canada described him thus:

> **Thrust into prominence for which he was ill-prepared by early training, and which would have dazed a feeble mind, Renforth grew to his new circumstances with gratifying rapidity. From being utterly uncouth, he became softened in manner and speech.**

Elliott's words about Renforth's widow suggest that she found the transition from being a smith's striker's wife to becoming the spouse of the champion sculler of the world problematic. But I do not think Mary Ann should be judged too harshly. Renforth himself had not always behaved as it was thought he should – remember his fall out with his backers Brown and Stewart, his assault on the waterman Maddison, and his move to the Sir Charles Napier Inn. He was the champion and received praise and support to assist him to progress socially and commercially, while his wife was largely ignored until she offended the sensibilities of the establishment. Let us remember that Mary Ann won her case, and that the personal criticism of her came from a man who was judged in law to have failed in his duty as a trustee. I would like to know more about the relationship between Renforth and his wife, but tantalisingly the evidence is not available. The court case over the missing £200 raises more questions than it answers and for the present the prudent biographer should refrain from speculation.

# Appendix 1
## Stakes, Side Bets and the Value of Money in 1870

Professional rowing during Renforth's time was not just about having the ability to defeat other oarsmen in order to collect big cash prizes. A share of the stake had to be raised for match races, and even to enter a regatta an entrance fee was required. The question then arises: if the same system was operating today, what sort of sums would we be talking about?

I have looked at a number of price indexes and cost of living statistics for the period, but I believe that the best way of illustrating the relative value of the money being wagered is with reference to the weekly wages of men working on Tyneside. Renforth and his fellow rowers came from within this community and these were the weekly amounts they could expect to bring home when they were not actively engaged in rowing.

In 1852 shipyard rivetters could be attracted to move from Glasgow to Tyneside by offering them 25 or 26 shillings a week (£1.25 or £1.30). Good, unskilled workers might make the switch for 19 shillings (£0.95). During an economic depression in 1884, the Wallsend Slipway labour force average annual earnings fell from £89 to £70. In 1886 shipyard workers on the river were earning the following weekly sums: Platers 33 shillings (£1.65); Rivetters and Caulkers 31 shillings (£1.55); Holders-up 25 shillings (£1.25).

It seems reasonable to reckon the average weekly wage for an unskilled manual worker in 1870 to be around a £1, and for a skilled man about 30 shillings (£1.50).

If one makes a comparison with wages today, one would need to multiply by at least 200. It is rather rough and ready but if you want to get an idea of the order of magnitude of stakes, side bets, prizes and entrance fees referred to in this book, I believe it works reasonably well.

As an example it can be seen that when Renforth fell out with his backers, early in 1868, he was unable to raise more than £10 as his share of the stake for an open boat race with John Bright. He did not have the money available from his own resources but obtained it from ordinary working men. The £10 would have represented between 7 and 10 weeks wages, a considerable sum, worth perhaps £2000 today, using our rule of thumb.

In November 1868, with the support of professional backers, Renforth's share of the stake for his match with Harry Kelley for the Championship of England was £200, the equivalent of £40,000 today.

# Appendix 2
# James Renforth 1842-1871: a chronology

**1842** 7th April. Born in New Pandon Street, in the Manors area of Newcastle upon Tyne, to Jane and James Renforth, who was a smith.

**1843** Family move to the Rabbit Banks-Pipewellgate area of Gateshead.

**1857** Joins an East India Company regiment and sails as part of the relieving force for the Indian Mutiny

**1859-1863**
Smith's striker at NER Engineering Works at Greenesfield, Gateshead; Tyne Port Authority, Howdon; and probably also in other works on both banks of the Tyne.

**1860** 23rd July. Joined Durham Royal Garrison Artillery at Gateshead.

**1860-1865**
Swimmer. Won a gold medal for swimming at Northumberland Baths. Walked to Talkin Tarn (near Carlisle, Cumbria) to take part in a swimming race. Lost.

**1861** 26th June. Marries Mary Ann Bell at Newcastle Register Office.

**1862** 29th June. Birth of daughter, Margaret Jane. Living at Dean Court, Newcastle upon Tyne.

**1863** 21st January. Death of daughter, Margaret Jane, from bronchitis. Living at Tuthill Stairs, Newcastle upon Tyne.

**1863** 21st December. Birth of daughter, Ann Elizabeth, in Lying In Hospital, New Bridge Street, Newcastle.

**1866** Employed in demolition of Old Tyne Bridge.

**1866** Debut against Robinson alias Princey. Won easily. Princey led but 'blew up'.

**1866** Saturday 19th May . Victory over G. Curry of Gateshead in open boats for £20.

**1867** Monday 22nd April. Race with Balmbra (or W. Bambrough) of Gateshead, in open boats for £20.Won.

**1867** Won heat in an open boat handicap at Talkin Tarn Regatta.

| 1867 | August. Beat Edward Boddy at Newcastle Swimming Club competition in the Tyne. Won a medal. |
|---|---|
| 1867 | 21st September. Beat Robert Boyd for £50 in open boats. |
| 1867 | 5th October. Beat James Boyd in skiffs for £100, High Level to Scotswood Suspension Bridge. |
| 1867 | 9th December. Should have rowed a skiff race against John Bright for £50 a side. Bright was unable to race because of illness and forfeited his £40 down. |
| 1868 | 28th March. Race with Bright in open boats for £20. Won easily. |
| 1868 | 23rd June. Birth of daughter, Margaret Jane, at the family home, 6 Church Street, Gateshead. |
| 1868 | 30th June at Durham Regatta. Won the Brancepeth Castle Plate defeating James Taylor and other local scullers. At same meeting, part of Albion R.C. second crew which was beaten in a race for the Patrons' Plate by the Champion Four. |
| 1868 | July. Leeds Regatta. Defeated by James Taylor in a handicap skiff race. Taylor had an allowance of two lengths. At the same regatta, on 14th July, Renforth won the Aire Stakes, value £25, and a local title of champion. |
| 1868 | 14th July. James present at death of daughter, Margaret Jane, from tabes (emaciation) at 6 Church Street, Gateshead. |
| 1868 | 4th August. Thames National Regatta. Won £90 in a skiff race in which Kelley, Sadler and Percy also competed. Tyne crews also won the fours and the pairs. Commemorated in the song, *Defeat of the Cocknies*. |
| 1868 | First public appearance in 'Champion Four' crew, Renforth (bow), M. Scott, A. Thompson, J. Taylor, J. French (cox), at the Chester Regatta where they won the Waterman's Prize of £40 with great ease. Renforth also won the Scullers' Prize of £10, beating James Taylor of Newcastle and Harry Lang of Manchester. |
| 1868 | Part of same crew which won the Town Purse of £30 at the Burton-on-Trent Regatta. |
| 1868 | 17th November. Beat Harry Kelley for the championship of the world on the Thames. |
| 1869 | Split in champion four-oared crew of which Renforth was a member. It was made up of Taylor, Renforth, Thompson and Scott. |

1869    6th January . Assault charge heard in Newcastle Court after attack on man in spirit bar. Found guilty and fined.

1869    25th January. Taylor and Renforth, in one boat, rowed against Thompson and Scott, in another, from bridge to bridge on the Tyne for £200. Renforth and Taylor won easily.

1869    5th May. Deserted from Durham RGA Militia.

1869    31st May. Pro-am race in pair oar boats. Renforth and Gulston against James Taylor and James Wallace. Lost.

1869    Wednesday 10th June. On scullers' race at King's Lynn Royal Regatta.

1869    Wednesday 14th July, Hartlepools' Regatta. Lost scullers race to James Boyd of Gateshead. In awkward sea conditions but arousing the suspicions of the crowd.

1869    Renforth and Taylor form a crew to compete at 1869 Thames National Regatta. These two plus Thomas Winship and John Martin.

1869    By early August Renforth is landlord of the Belted Will Inn, Hinde Street, Scotswood Rd.

1869    Thursday 5th August, Chester Regatta. Won Watermen's Sculls (£7) beating James Taylor and Thomas Winship. Next day Renforth's crew won Watermen's Fours (£40).

1869    Friday 6th August, Wear Boat Club Regatta. Renforth and Taylor win pairs (£5) as they please. Renforth wins skiff race (£8) in *Adelaide*.

1869    Saturday 21st August, Thames Regatta. Above-mentioned four beaten by Surbiton crew. Tyne crew challenge Surbiton crew to race twice more, once on the Thames and once on the Tyne, for £400 each race.

1869    5th and 6th October. Renforth rows against Bright for £100 a-side in open boats from High Level Bridge to Meadows House. Bright getting two lengths start in $1^3/_4$ miles. Foul on first day leading to re-row. Foul again but decision given to Bright. After the race on the 6th Renforth collapses in a fit in the bar of the Star Hotel, Northumberland Street, Newcastle and is taken home in a cab.

1869    Tyne four-oar crew win both races against Surbiton crew. November 5th on Thames and 18th November on Tyne.

1869    Two days after the match on the Tyne, 20th November, Renforth and Taylor are beaten in a double scull race for £200 with Kelley and Sadler on the Tyne from bridge to bridge.

1870    February. Moves from Belted Will Inn to take over as landlord of Sir Charles Napier Inn, Queen Street, St Nicholas' Buildings.

1870    5th July. Wins Brancepeth Plate (scullers race) and Patrons Plate (as part of Champion Four) at Durham Regatta.

1870    Sunday 17th July. Pall bearer at Harry Clasper's funeral.

1870    September. Renforth's crew (Renforth, James Taylor, Thomas Winship, John Martin, with John Adams as spare man) defeat Canadians at Lake Lachine, Canada.

1871    16th January. Renforth and Kelley beat James Taylor and Thomas Winship in a pair-oar race on the Tyne for £400.

1871    Sells Sir Charles Napier Inn.

1871    Thursday 15th June, Tyne Regatta. Renforth and Kelley beaten by James Taylor and Thomas Winship in pairs. Kelley suffering from sciatica and rowing against medical advice. Renforth's crew, Renforth, Kelley, Chambers, Percy, Bright (spare) which was formed to go out to Canada, has to be reorganised because of Kelley's indisposition. Friday 16th June, Renforth, Bright, Chambers, Percy beat Taylor's crew in fours.

1871    Wednesday 23rd August. Death of Renforth, after collapsing during race against Canadians at St John, New Brunswick.

1871    Sunday 10th September. Funeral of Renforth and burial in Gateshead Cemetery. Funeral procession starts from Renforth's house in James Street, Gateshead, which he probably bought after the sale of the Sir Charles Napier Inn earlier in the year.

1872    Monday late October. Inauguration of Renforth Memorial.

1884    19th May. Court Case at Newcastle County Court concerning whereabouts of £200 due to Renforth's daughter, Ann Elizabeth now married and called Heler. Case found in favour of daughter and widow Mary Ann, now remarried to William John Renforth (James Renforth's cousin).

# Bibliography

## Contemporary Newspapers

*Newcastle Daily Chronicle; Newcastle Daily Journal; Gateshead Observer; Gateshead Post; The Gateshead Times; Illustrated London News; South Durham and Cleveland Mercury; South Durham Herald*

## Books and later publications

Ayris, Ian and Jubb, Peter, *A Guide to the Public Monuments and Sculpture of Tyne and Wear*, Newcastle, 1996.

Clark, J.F., *Building Ships on the North East Coast, Part 1 c1640-1914*, Bewick Press, Tyne and Wear, 1997.

Clasper, David, *Harry Clasper Hero of the North*, Gateshead, 1990.

Dillon, Peter, *The Tyne Oarsmen*, Newcastle, 1993.

Dodd, Christopher, *The Oxford and Cambridge Boat Race*, London, 1983.

Dodd, Christopher, *The Story of World Rowing*, London, 1992.

Ermel, Trevor, and Carnaffin, Eileen, *The Changing Face of Gateshead*, Gateshead, 1992.

Hale, John R., 'The Lost Technology of Ancient Greek Rowing', In *Scientific American* p66-71, May 1976.

Halladay, Eric, *Rowing in England: A Social History. The Amateur Debate*, Manchester University Press, 1992.

Hanscombe, Alice, and Hughes, Liz, *Epilepsy*, Ward Lock, London, 1995.

Lathers, Claire M., and Schraeder, Paul L. (eds), *Epilepsy and Sudden Death*, Marcel Dekker Inc, New York, 1990.

Manders, F.W.D., *Gateshead in Times Past*, Chorley, Lancashire, 1979.

McCord, Norman, *British History 1815-1906*, Oxford University Press. 1991.

McCord, Norman, and Thompson, Richard, *The Northern Counties from AD 1000*, Longman, London, 1998.

Phelps Brown, E.H., *A Century of Pay 1860-1960*, Macmillan, London, 1968.

Sampson, Aylwin, *Winning Waters*, Hale, London, 1986.

Temkin, Owsei, *The Falling Sickness: A History of Epilepsy from the Greeks to the Beginnings of Modern Neurology* (2nd edition), The John Hopkins Press, Baltimore, 1971.

Vamplew, Wray, *Pay up and Play the Game: Professional Sport in Britain 1875-1914*, Cambridge University Press, 1988.

Wilson, Joe, *Tyneside Songs and Drolleries,* Republished by S.R. Publishers Ltd., Wakefield, 1970.

Wright, Alan, *Tom Sayers, The Last Great Bare-Knuckle Champion*, The Book Guild Ltd., Sussex, 1994.

# Illustrations

# INDEX